The Way to Deeper Love

PRAYING
FOR (& WITH)
YOUR
SPOUSE

The Way to Deeper Love

PRAYING FOR (& WITH) YOUR SPOUSE

Dr. Greg and Lisa Popcak

the WORD among us® press

Published by The Word Among Us Press
7115 Guilford Drive, Suite 100
Frederick, Maryland 21704
wau.org

22 21 20 19 18   1 2 3 4 5

ISBN: 978-1-59325-331-8
eISBN: 978-1-59325-506-0

Cover design by Faceout Studio, Tim Green
Cover Photograph by Stocksy Images

Made and printed in the United States of America

Library of Congress Control Number: 2018932959

Contents

Part One

Tapping into the Spiritual
Power of Your Marriage

CHAPTER ONE

The Spiritual Power of Marriage

Marriage is filled with a million grace-filled moments that connect us to God, open our hearts in surprising ways, and challenge and transform us. What grace-filled moments are hidden in plain sight in *your* marriage? To give you an idea of what we mean, here are a few examples of the stories we have collected over the years from couples for whom, time and again, God used the spiritual power of their marriage to reveal his love and grace in wonderful and surprising ways.

"The other day, Karen looked at me in that way she does. I saw myself in her eyes, and I felt so . . . grateful. I thought to myself, 'There has to be a God, because no one could ever love me the way she does if there wasn't.'"

"When I was growing up, my family was pretty awful. I was afraid to get married for a long time, because I didn't want to trust my heart to someone who could hurt me like that ever again. But Jim is like no other man I've ever met. I've never felt so safe and cared for by anyone. He made it possible for me to open up in ways I never thought I'd be able to. God is using my marriage to bring about all kinds of healing in my heart. I mean, it isn't always easy, but I can't think of a moment I'm not grateful."

"I've always been kind of a worrywart. I tend to panic over all the unexpected stuff— unexpected bills, sickness, unpleasant news—big, little, it doesn't matter. As you can imagine, I'm anxious a lot of the time, and it's taken real work to get a handle on it. But over the twenty years Ken and I have been together, I can see how much more peaceful I am than when we first got married. Honestly, I'm like a different person compared to how I was then. I look back at all the things we've been through together—all the times I thought, 'This is it. This is where it all comes crashing down.' And I see how God has gotten us through so much. I'm still more nervous than I'd like, but I have a hard time getting really worked up these days, like I used to, because I see how faithful God has been over the years, and I know that I just have to trust him. God has used my marriage to help me experience a peace I never thought I'd have."

"When Jack and I had our first child, God touched my heart in such a powerful way. I felt so full of love for my daughter, and it dawned on me that as much as I love my child, God loves me so much more. It's hard to even imagine, but as I looked at her little face, I was so filled up with love. It was probably the first time I really felt—to that degree—how much God must love me. It took my relationship with God to a whole new level."

"When Elizabeth got cancer, I was so angry. I was mad at God for not protecting her, at myself for working so hard all those years and missing out on the healthy times, at her for getting sick when I was finally feeling like maybe I could step away from work enough to start enjoying our life together a little more. All my life, I guess I was what you might call a 'Sunday Christian.' I'd go to church with Elizabeth on the weekend, if I didn't have something better to do, but I never thought much about God during the week. But through that whole horrible year, that all changed. Every chance I got, I begged God for another chance to be the man I should have been all along.

I wouldn't wish her diagnosis on anyone, but God used it to change me, as well as our marriage, in some amazing ways. Everything shifted. He refocused me on loving her, on being there for her in ways I never had the courage to be there for her before. Thanks be to God, she's been in remission for a couple of years now, and her health looks good, but we're both totally different people. God is the center of our marriage now, and I can't tell you what a difference he's made in our hearts and in our home. It breaks my heart to hear Elizabeth say that getting here was worth all the suffering she endured. I wish it didn't take all that. But I know she's right, and we're both so grateful to God."

Can you think of moments when God has touched your heart through your marriage? Note some of these times here:

God of the Everyday

Sometimes we experience God's grace *because* of our mate, and sometimes, even in the best of marriages, we experience God's grace *in spite* of our mate. But God is always reaching out to us, calling us, loving us, strengthening us, and changing us through the gift of marriage. Marriage is more than just a guarantee we will always have our *plus one* at the ready. Marriage has real spiritual power, and we can learn how to tap into that power so that marriage can fulfill the mission all the sacraments were ordained to fulfill: perfect us in Christ and lead us into a deeper, intimate encounter with him.

And yet, like Martha (see Luke 10:38-42), today's husbands and wives are busy with so many things. It becomes easy to forget that God is hidden behind every moment of our married lives. We can forget to look for him. But when we pray for and with our spouse, God reminds us of the powerful ways he is revealing himself in all the little intimate moments between husbands and wives: in the hugs and kisses, the knowing glances, the conflicts and worries, the new challenges and opportunities; for better and for worse, richer and poorer, in sickness and in health, in good times and bad. God takes all of this and consecrates it, allowing each husband and wife, through their married love, to "rise 'in ecstasy' towards the Divine."[1]

Pope Francis commented that marriage is "God's icon, created for us by He who is the perfect communion of the three Persons; the Father, the Son and the Holy Spirit."

The love of the Trinity and Christ's love for his bride, the Church, must therefore be "the focus of marriage catechesis and evangelization."[2]

We grant you that all this represents some high-level thinking about marriage, but it speaks directly to its practical, spiritual power. In particular, this means that God wants to use marriage to satisfy the deep longing that every person experiences for a love that doesn't fail—a love that reflects the generous, faithful, fruitful, and unfailing love that the Father, Son, and Holy Spirit have for each other.

Further, marriage shows us that God doesn't love us from a distance—he is present and concerned in every single moment of our lives. He loves us in and through the joys and struggles of our daily life. He loves us through all the mundane moments and monotony and all the drama and joy. There isn't any part of our lives that God doesn't wish to set ablaze with the fire of his love, from the way we do dishes together to the way we raise our kids with each other to the ways we express our passion and desire for one another. Our marriages can witness to the fact that God is the God of the everyday, the God who doesn't think that any part of our lives is unworthy of his time and care.

Married couples can be beacons, shining from the windows of their homes, reminding aching hearts that the love they long for, the love the world says isn't possible, is *real*. As we regularly remind listeners of our radio program, being faithful to your spouse in a faithless world, remaining committed to your spouse in a world that is allergic to commitment, working to stay in love with each other over the years in a world that says that love always dies—this is your witness; this is a ministry that can transform hearts.

Marriage has the power to reveal all of this because, as Scripture and Church teaching make clear, God's own relationship with the Church—with each of us in the Church—is like the relationship between a bridegroom and bride.

Be Exactly Who You Are

The good news? You don't have to be anywhere near perfect to accomplish all that God has for you. You can be that imperfect husband and wife who sometimes say things you regret or who argue about who drives better and who should take out the dog or attend to the baby. You can even be that couple who went through that time (or ten) when you really weren't sure you were going to make it, but somehow (hint, hint—grace) you did. If you want to tap the spiritual power of your marriage and allow God to take your relationship to the next level, you don't have to be anything other than exactly who you are, as long as you do one simple thing: pray for and with your spouse.

That is the secret. God wants to give you everything you lack, so that you can be the couple you dreamed of becoming when you first fell in love. God will help you celebrate your joys more boldly and your love more passionately. Your discussions can become more productive and your partnership more fruitful. You can learn to manage your conflicts in a way that helps you fall more in love with each other *because of* your disagreements rather than in spite of them. Your kids and your grandkids, seeing your love, will want to be like you when they grow up.

These are the blessings of a great love that is rooted in God's love. This is the kind of love that sets the world on fire for Christ. And it all begins with praying for and with your spouse.

The other day, we received an interesting bit of news. We had a guest on our radio program from the United States Conference of Catholic Bishops' Office for Laity, Marriage, Family, and Youth. She said that her office recently ran an Internet poll at their popular site, ForYourMarriage.org, asking readers to name couples who inspired them to have a great, godly marriage. A number of respondents mentioned "the Popcaks" as the couple who inspired them the most. One respondent wrote, "Mary and Joseph and the Popcaks." We nearly choked on that one. Talk about intimidating!

We share this story not to spread the word about our awesomeness but rather to bear witness to what God can do with two genuinely stupid, broken, and struggling people like us. The truth is, we do have an enviable marriage—praise God!—but it is not false modesty to say that if he can do it for us, he will certainly have a much easier time doing it for you. As we share in our book *Just Married: The Catholic Guide to Surviving and Thriving in the First Five Years of Marriage*, there is no reason our marriage should have made it out of the gate, much less been able to inspire anyone to anything (other than to avoid marriage altogether).

We got engaged after two months of dating. We were married the day after our college graduation. Our families and friends all thought we were crazy, and of course, we were. Greg's mother even stopped speaking to him for a while to protest our engagement.

We had nothing. We had no jobs, no money, little support, and less sense. In the first five years of our marriage, we dealt with two car crashes, life-threatening illnesses, a miscarriage, financial struggles, graduate school, and constant exhaustion. Looking back, there were absolutely no rational criteria by which we should have made it. In fact, we could have checked just about every box for poster children of "kids whose marriage will never work."

Neither of us saw phenomenal marriages growing up. Lisa's dad died when she was five, and her mother never remarried. Greg's parents cared for each other and hung in there for life, but they struggled a lot. When Greg was a child of six or seven, for example, his parents fought so much one night that he put on his plastic army helmet, got his toy canon, and stood guard outside his parents' bedroom door to prevent his mother from leaving the house when he heard her threaten divorce. He remembers keeping his armed vigil on more than one occasion as his parents fought in the next room, thinking Greg was asleep when he was anything but. Fortunately, Greg's parents made it through that time, largely because of their faith.

All of this makes the point that neither of us experienced blissful models of effortless marriage growing up. If there is anything inspiring about our marriage today, it is in spite of who we are and where we came from, not because of it.

Looking back almost thirty years, we can confidently say that there was one thing, and one thing only, that helped us create the kind of marriage that satisfies the deepest longings of our hearts and—by some miracle—serves as an encouragement to others. That is the fact that from the very first day we started dating, we began praying for and with each other. All along, we asked God to take our relationship and make it what he wanted it to be. First, we brought our friendship to him, and then our love, then our engagement, and now, together, we bring every day of our married life to him.

In return, God is taking two stumbling, stupid kids and teaching us, step-by-step, how to love each other with the love that flows from his heart. Today, because we both continue to be very much works in progress, he is still teaching us, and by his grace, he will continue to do so until the day we meet him face-to-face, at the eternal wedding feast. In the words of St. Paul,

> *God chose the foolish of the world to shame the wise. . . . It is due to him that you are in Christ Jesus, who became for us wisdom from God, as well as righteousness, sanctification, and redemption, so that, as it is written, "Whoever boasts, should boast in the Lord." (1 Corinthians 1:27, 30-31)*

If there is anything good about our marriage, it is there because God has given it to us. We are proud to boast in him. That said, we can promise you that he will be more than happy to give you everything you need as well, and more. Why? Because he loves you, of course, but also because your love for one another reflects the greatest love story of all, the story of the love between Jesus Christ and his bride, the Church. Your married love, therefore, helps to further God's plan for the world.

We invite you to walk with us on this journey, learning how to tap into the spiritual power of your marriage by praying for and with your spouse. Throughout this book, you will discover how you can consecrate each part of your married life to God and draw on the spiritual power that flows like a river of grace beneath the surface of your heart. Are you ready to see the amazing things God wants to do in you and in your home?

Then let's get to it!

CHAPTER TWO

Prayer, the Key to Unlocking the Spiritual Power of Marriage

Prayer—especially praying with your spouse—can seem intimidating. To make the whole experience more user-friendly, this chapter will look at prayer in general. How can you get the most out of prayer, whether you do it on your own or with your husband or wife? And how do prayer and marriage go together?

Nothing Goes to Waste

Marriage is a sacrament and a vocation. That's true, of course, and it's lovely to say, but what does it mean? And what difference does it make to your prayer life?

The fact that marriage is both a sacrament and your vocation means that God can use every part of your relationship to communicate with you, reveal himself to you, heal you, transform you, and raise you up into the saint he is calling you to be. Nothing about your marriage is wasted, as far as God is concerned: not your arguments, not the boring stuff involved in managing your everyday life, and certainly not the joys and pleasures of married love. God invites you and your spouse not only to pray for and with one another but also to view your married life as a prayer that facilitates deeper communion with God.

Many couples might find this an odd thing to say, at the very least. Even many committed Christians do not experience the spiritual-marital dynamic we have described so far. But this isn't a novel concept. Scripture and Church teaching both present marriage as a means for a couple to grow in holiness. In truth, the grace is there for every couple to experience their marriage as a deeply soulful instrument of grace and growth.

But in order to experience the spiritual power of marriage, we need to connect every part of our marriage to the pipeline of grace, prayer. Prayer is a conversation with God, but it is even more than that. St. John Vianney once said, "Prayer is nothing less than union with God."[3] When you combine these two notions of prayer—conversation and union— you discover that praying for and with your spouse means entering into a regular conversation with your spouse *and* God, through which you receive grace to enter into deeper communion with both. Praying for and with your spouse allows you to discover, in a personal and powerful way, that prayer brings you into deeper relational and spiritual intimacy with your mate and the God who gave you to each other in his love.

BFF's in the Beginning

The Book of Genesis describes how, in the beginning, before original sin entered the world, Adam and Eve enjoyed what Pope St. John Paul the Great referred to as "original unity;"[4] that is, they were perfectly united with God and each other. This perfect union allowed them to truly "get" each other. To be perfect helpmates to each other. To never feel used by each other. To always work for each other's good in every aspect of their relationship. To truly be godly BFF's (best friends forever). And finally, to see every moment of their life together as an opportunity to draw closer to each other and to God.

Of course, since the Fall, the relationship between man, woman, and God has become . . . complicated. That's where prayer can make a difference. Husbands and wives who pray for and with each other open themselves more intentionally to the graces of marriage. They might even find themselves enjoying something of the unity God originally intended for men and women, evident in the pre-fallen union of Adam and Eve—at least to the degree that this is possible on this side of heaven.

In our experience, many Christians—and Catholics in particular—struggle to have the kind of meaningful prayer lives that could make this beautiful ideal a reality for their relationships. Studies show that most Catholics pray almost every day, but for some, prayer is often an awkward struggle to figure out what to say and how to act. Others have very committed and dutiful prayer lives but struggle to encounter God *as a person* or to experience much transformation in their lives or relationships as a result of their prayer. Still others think of prayer as a kind of spiritual vacation from their troubles, a quiet time of rote prayer and familiar formulas that gives comfort but rarely provides opportunities for transformation or deeper intimacy.

In the course of our ministry, we have met many people who have prayed in these ways for years, even decades. And they are genuinely surprised to learn that relating to God in a personal way, hearing him "talk back" in prayer, and receiving grace to make positive, practical changes in their lives and relationships are normal and expected parts of a healthy prayer life.

To be fair, all of the above experiences of prayer are genuine, sincere, and laudable starting points. We do not mean to be critical of anyone's approach to or experience of prayer. Just as God does not waste any part of your marriage, he celebrates any effort you make to reach out to him. But if, up to now, your experience of prayer has been awkward or primarily dutiful, then think of the following pages as an invitation to take your prayer life to the next level.

Prayer: A User's Guide

Traditionally there are three different kinds (or "degrees") of prayer: vocal prayer, meditative prayer, and contemplative prayer.

Vocal Prayer

By definition, vocal prayer—the way we pray most often—involves words said either out loud or interiorly. Vocal prayer can consist of formal prayers, like the Rosary and the Our Father, or informal prayers that we offer in our own words, like little conversations with God.

Vocal prayer can incorporate praise, through which we celebrate the ways we experience the goodness of God himself. For example, "Lord, you are so merciful, so loving, so glorious." Or we can offer thanksgiving, through which we celebrate the things God has done for us. For example, "Thank you, Lord, for helping me find a way to pay that unexpected bill!" We can intercede for the needs of others or for our own needs. We can seek God's forgiveness for the harm we have caused and ask for the grace to do better in the future.

As you can see, vocal prayer covers a lot of ground. Because it is so versatile, it lends itself to group prayer, and you will probably find yourself using it a lot as you pray for and with your spouse. For instance, you might pray a Rosary or a Divine Mercy Chaplet together for the intention of a godlier, more grace-filled marriage (formal vocal prayer), or you could just talk to God about your day together (informal vocal prayer).

Together with your spouse, you might *praise* God for giving you his love as a model to follow in learning to love each other better, and you could *thank* him for the specific blessings of that day or the specific ways he has blessed each of you through your relationship. You might engage in *supplication,* asking God's help in meeting a specific need, such as, "Lord, please help our son's broken leg heal quickly and without any need for surgery." Or you might *intercede* for a couple you know who is struggling with concerns of their own.

You might even ask for God's forgiveness when you let each other down: "Lord, please forgive us for snapping at each other all day today. We really let the stress get to us. Please give us the grace to handle better everything we go through tomorrow and to remember to be loving to each other in the midst of it all."

Throughout this book, we will suggest different ways to use vocal prayer to strengthen your relationship. For now it's enough to point out that it is a great method of prayer for couples who want to seek God's blessings for their relationship. In the space below, jot down some examples of how you (alone or with your spouse) already use vocal prayer in your marriage.

_____

_____

_____

_____

_____

Meditative Prayer

Meditative prayer usually involves reflecting on a focal point—such as a Scripture verse, a holy image, a biblical story or a story from the life of a saint, or a certain repeated sacred word or phrase—as a way of entering into a deeper relationship with God. When people first learn to pray the Rosary, for example, they often pray it as a vocal prayer by simply "saying" their Rosary. The Church, however, teaches us that the Rosary is meant to be a kind of meditative prayer.

Ideally, we should pray the Rosary in a manner that allows us to enter into the mysteries of Christ's life, passion, death, and resurrection, to reflect on what those things mean for us personally, in the here and now. Our hands hold the beads, and our mouths repeat the words, but our minds and hearts are meant to soar above those physical anchors into the deeper mysteries of the life of God and his relationship with us. If you pray the joyful mysteries in this manner, for example, you might reflect on what it must have been like for Mary when the angel Gabriel told her that she would conceive the Son of God. Then consider what her response—"May it be done to me according to your word" (Luke 1:38)—means for your own response to God's call. Or reflecting on the sorrowful mysteries, consider that God's love for you led him to endure the cross— and perhaps he is calling you to respond with sacrificial love to a particular circumstance in your own life.

Anyone who has prayed the Rosary in this way knows that this is a very different experience of prayer than saying a bunch of Hail Marys as quickly as possible in order to check "prayer" off the day's to-do list. Whether with the Rosary or Scripture or other means, meditative prayer uses items, words, and rituals to focus our minds and bodies so that God can reveal himself in a deeper way. The following examples will give you some ideas about how to bring meditative prayer into your marriage.

In using the Rosary as a tool for meditative prayer *in your marriage*, you might reflect, as you pray together, on the ways in which each mystery calls you to respond more gracefully to your spouse or to the challenges in your marriage. As you pray the sorrowful mysteries, for instance, you might consider how much God loves each of you— and continues to call out to you—even when you frustrate his call or his plans for you.

You could also take a moment at the end of the Rosary— or at the end of each decade—to briefly share your reflections with one another. As you are praying the joyful mysteries together, for example, you could reflect on the anxiety Mary must have felt at the Annunciation and then mention your own hopes or concerns about having a child.

Lectio divina (literally, "divine reading") is a type of Scripture-based prayer that can be used effectively when praying with your spouse. In this type of meditative prayer, you choose a Scripture verse or passage and sit quietly with it, praying about it and seeing how God might wish to speak to you through it.

To practice divine reading in your marriage, you might choose a verse from Scripture that uses wedding imagery, such as the story of the wedding feast at Cana (see John 2:1-12). Read it alone or together, and then reflect together on why God chose a wedding as the occasion of his first miracle. What might this say about the dignity of marriage and its importance as a sacrament? You might even reflect on how God is calling you to love each other more, or differently, in light of this example. You might consider how you and your spouse can be his light in the world by the way you love each other and strive together to be faithful, even during difficult times.

There are many other passages of Scripture that speak directly to married love or can be applied to married love. The Book of Hosea, for example, is an extended reflection on God's faithfulness to an undeserving Israel told through the lens of the prophet Hosea's anguished relationship with his unfaithful wife, Gomer. The Song of Songs is a provocative reflection on God's passionate love for his people seen through the lens of two young lovers' passionate desire for one another. There are many references to marriage and family life in the various epistles of St. Paul and other books of the New Testament.

You can also use meditative prayer to reflect together on the different images the Church uses when speaking about marriage. For example, you might choose to meditate on why the Church says that marriage represents a relationship between Christ and the Church—the Bridegroom and the bride. Or why the crucifixion is spoken of as the "nuptials" that wedded heaven and earth. Or why the Church speaks of marriage as an icon of the Trinity. This last image might help you and your spouse reflect on how the Father, Son, and Holy Spirit relate to each other and might suggest ways you can imitate that love in your married life.

Contemplative Prayer

We never pray on our own. Christians believe that if we are praying, it is because, on some level, God is moving in us and calling us to himself. Even the simplest act of vocal prayer is impossible unless God first moves in us and gives us the grace to turn our hearts and minds to him. Perhaps we recognize this action of God most profoundly in contemplative prayer, which can unfold as a powerful encounter with God that exceeds words but fills up every part of us. These powerful sacred moments can give even simple things deep meaning.

Experiences of contemplative prayer can result in significant growth in wisdom and a deeper, more personal connection with God. They can even be life changing. In a sense, contemplative prayer is when God grabs our attention and says, "Look at this! I want to show you something." Saints like Teresa of Avila, Catherine of Siena, and Bernard of Clairvaux, to name just a few, were mystics who experienced God revealing himself in powerful ways during contemplative prayer. These were sacred moments that were deeply significant and profoundly felt. They were sources of great insights about the nature of God and his relationship to humanity.

It would be possible to come away from this discussion thinking that contemplative prayer is either an entirely passive enterprise that we wait for or something that only spiritual masters experience. Neither is true.

Contemplative prayer often represents the most dramatic way God speaks with us in the unitive conversation that is prayer, and there is much that we can do to ready our hearts and minds to hear his voice. Because contemplative prayer is, in a sense, active, it begins with quieting our minds and turning our hearts to the Lord, so that we might be ready to receive whatever he wants to share with us, whenever he wants to share it.

The more we participate in the call that God places on our hearts through vocal and meditative prayer, the easier it is for him to get our attention. He will point out things we might not notice were it not for his taking our face in his hands and saying, "Look!"

Perhaps you have had moments when you just *knew* something to be undeniably true—maybe about God's love for you or what he is asking you to do. For whatever reason, you came away from that moment utterly convinced that this was of God, and nothing and no one could shake your belief that you had experienced something real, something powerful, something that was perhaps beyond words but also a source of many future insights and blessings in your life. Contemplative prayer can be like that.

If you haven't had experiences like these, don't worry. If you stay faithful and open to the movement of the Holy Spirit in your prayer life, it is very likely that you will. God loves you so much. He wants you to know his love on every level. And part of the way he demonstrates his love is through sacred moments of transcendence that characterize the experience of what Christians call contemplative prayer. If you have already had experiences like these or are familiar with such experiences in the lives of the saints, write of an example below of how God reached out and "spoke back" in a powerful and unmistakable way.

————————————————————————
————————————————————————
————————————————————————
————————————————————————
————————————————————————
————————————————————————

Contemplative Prayer in Marriage:
A Loving Look

Couples can enter into contemplative prayer as they grow in their prayer life together, opening their hearts to him, cultivating a sense of his presence both during prayer and outside of prayer. These moments of powerful encounters with God's love can spill over into everyday life.

Greg likes to share about a time he caught Lisa looking at him in a particularly loving way. As Lisa looked at him, he had an intense flash in which he felt God saying, "Look at how much I love you. Can you believe that I gave you this amazing woman who loves you this much? Well, I love you even more!"

Greg has had many experiences of God's love in his lifetime, but there was something that stood out about this one powerful moment, which he says he won't ever forget. It is difficult for him to put it into words, but it was significant because it resulted in his deeper understanding of many of the things we are discussing here—particularly that marriage isn't just an earthly gift to make this life better but a real and powerful sign of how much God loves every part of us and uses every part of our lives to draw us into his very own heart.

Lisa tells a story of a time when she, too, unexpectedly felt God's intense love for her—the sort of love that can be felt in contemplative prayer. We were going through a particularly difficult situation that resulted in months of scary moments and sleepless nights. Lisa had been praying for weeks for some kind of consolation without feeling any peace in any part of her life, her prayer life in particular. One day she was making lunch for the kids. They had requested peanut butter sandwiches, and she was sure we were out of peanut butter. As she went to the pantry, one of the kids piped up, "God, could we please have peanut butter for lunch?"

At first Lisa was annoyed. She just wasn't in the mood, and it seemed like a silly thing to pray about. She almost told the kids to knock it off, but then she opened the pantry door and saw, out of the corner of her eye, an unopened jar of peanut butter buried in the back of the panty. She started to tear up.

"It sounds silly, but in that moment, I felt God saying, 'I've got you.' After all those weeks of asking God for something to hold onto, I felt he focused my attention on that stupid jar of peanut butter and told me, in the deepest part of my heart, if he cared so much about my kids getting what they wanted for lunch that day, what reason did I have to worry about his seeing us through this time?"

Although the situation dragged on for several more months, Lisa didn't worry as much from that point forward.

Anytime she started to worry, she remembered that jar of peanut butter and the verse from Scripture, "If you then, who are wicked, know how to give good gifts to your children, how much more will your heavenly Father give good things to those who ask him" (Matthew 7:11)?

You can experience contemplative prayer in and through your marriage. For now it is enough to know that marital contemplative prayer involves recognizing (1) that God wants to communicate something to you about his inner life and his relationship with you through your relationship with your spouse; and (2) that in your prayer life, you should continually ask God to open your heart to the ways he is using every part of your marriage—good times and bad, sickness and health, wealth and poverty—to speak to you. Incline your ear to listen for when and how he is speaking. Cultivating a contemplative mindset toward your marriage means prayerfully tuning your spiritual antennae to the grace that is always hiding, right below the surface of every mundane moment of your marriage, and filling your heart and home with God's presence and blessing beyond measure.

These are all pretty highfalutin concepts, and it can seem crazy to think that God would want to use marriage—of all things—to help us understand them. But God *does* want us to understand, and so he gives us concrete things, like marriage and family life, that at least give us hints of who he really is, how he "thinks," and how he relates to us. What can our marriage possibly teach us about the inner life of God? The Church tells us the answer is "a whole lot!"

As we go through this book, we'll share more examples of ways in which prayer can enrich your marriage and your relationship with God. For now, think about some simple ways you might start using meditative and contemplative prayer in your marriage. Or, if you already are using them, consider how you could improve and strengthen your practice. Write your reflections in the space below.

_____

_____

_____

_____

_____

Onward Ho!

Your marriage is much more than a source of earthly comfort and friendship. It is a spiritual dynamo, a powerhouse, a gift like no other. No matter what type of prayer you find most comfortable and familiar, the more you integrate prayer into your marriage, the more you will discover this power and see what a gift your marriage can be to those around you.

You will also learn that, although you need to set aside time to pray, you won't need to continually leave your marriage and family life to go pray: God will come to you *through* your marriage and family life. As we said in the beginning of this chapter, God wants to make sure no part of your marriage and family life is wasted. He wants to use everything—your blessings, your joys, your struggles, your arguments, your bedroom, even your laundry—to bring you into a deeper experience of his love for you.

You don't have to be a spiritual master or have a theology degree to make any of this happen. You just have to make the effort to bring your marriage to him in whatever simple ways you can, but first in prayer. As Pope Benedict XVI said in his catechesis on prayer,

> *Prayer as a way of "accustoming" oneself to being with God brings into being men and women who are not motivated by selfishness, by the desire to possess or by the thirst for power, but by gratuitousness, by the desire to love, by the thirst to serve, in other words who are motivated by God; and only in this way is it possible to bring light to the darkness of the world.*[5]

CHAPTER THREE

Praying for Your Spouse: Helpful Habits for Marital Intercession

You might be tempted to think, "A whole *chapter* on praying for your spouse? *Really?*" After all, praying for your husband or wife is no great mystery. How difficult is it to pray, "Lord, could you please make my spouse a *little* less annoying?"

It's OK. You can laugh. We've all prayed that. You know you have.

Of course, as we mentioned earlier, God welcomes all of our attempts to reach out to him, especially the heartfelt ones. And we know from experience that there are few more heartfelt prayers than the one above. Still, if you'd like to get even a tiny bit more from your prayer life as a husband or wife, this chapter on cultivating healthy habits for a deeper experience of marital intercessory prayer is for you.

Once we get past the inclination to limit our prayers for our spouse to requests that God help them realize that we were right and they were wrong, we discover that there is more to our marital intercession than meets the eye. Let's explore a few habits that, with a little practice, can help you get the most out of praying for your spouse and help you experience God's grace in your home like never before.

Step One: Begin with Gratitude

*In all circumstances give thanks, for this is the will of God
for you in Christ Jesus. (1 Thessalonians 5:18)*

It is important to begin every prayer in a spirit of gratitude.
God gives us so much. Every breath we take is a gift from
the Lord. So is each moment with our spouse.

Sometimes we feel grateful for our spouse, and sometimes we don't, but whether we do or not, our marriage
truly is a gift. In good times, marriage is one of the most
important ways God shows his love for us. If we are feeling
loved and cared for by our mate, we are really experiencing
God loving us and caring for us through our mate. Christian husbands and wives are God's good servants. When
we give wonderful love, support, comfort, and encouragement to each other, we are only delivering what the King
gave us in the first place.

When you begin to pray for your marriage in general or
your spouse in particular, take a moment to thank God for
the love that you share and the joy that you give to each
other. A simple "Thank you, Lord, for the love you have
given my spouse and me. Thank you for this marriage and
all the ways you show me your love through it!" can be
sufficient, although you should always feel free to use your
own words and expand on this as you are able. Remind
yourself that all the good things you share in your relationship and all the good things you hope to share with

each other truly come from God. Praise the Lord for giving you the grace to create this life together

Reflection Questions

- What things are you most grateful for in your relationship with your spouse? Are you in the habit of thanking God for these marital blessings?
- How could you ramp up your expressions of gratitude, both to your spouse and to God?

It's especially important to thank God for our spouse when we feel frustrated, disappointed, or angry with them. If that sounds a bit ridiculous, we don't mean that you should try to convince yourself that the problems you are going through are some kind of blessing in disguise. There is nothing wrong with admitting—to yourself, to your spouse, and to God—that your problems are, well, problematic. The biblical call to "give thanks" is not a call to slap a smiley face on problems and pretend things are OK when they are not. God is not glorified in our denial of reality. He is glorified in our ability to respond to our reality in graceful ways, to face our challenges with confidence, and to bring our best selves to our struggles, so that we can grow through them and, with his grace, overcome them.

Giving thanks for your spouse and marriage even in difficult times means intentionally calling to mind a few things. For example, recall that times haven't always been this tough. Research shows that people respond better to present problems when they can recall times they have felt stronger and happier than they currently do. Taking a moment to thank God for happier times—times when we felt closer to our spouse and times when we felt more resourceful than we currently do—isn't intended to distract us from handling the problems in front of us. Rather, it helps us realize that our marriage truly is worth the effort of applying ourselves to this present struggle; that God has always come through for us when we have leaned on him before, and we shouldn't start doubting him now; and finally, that, even in trial, God is present and blessing us in a million ways that deserve to be acknowledged.

Finding sincere ways to give God praise in times of trial is what St. Paul refers to as making a "sacrifice of praise" (Hebrews 13:15). We always thought that was a strange phrase. How can praise be a sacrifice? Well, if you've ever been through hard times in your life or marriage, you know what a sacrifice of praise can feel like. It isn't, as Tevye of *Fiddler on the Roof* proclaimed, that "God would like us to be joyful, even when our hearts lie panting on the floor."[6] Rather, focusing our minds on all the ways that God is blessing us even in trials strengthens us to carry on and gracefully respond to the challenges that are in front of us.

Another way to thank God in times of trial is to be grateful for the opportunity to grow stronger and more trusting through the challenges you face. For instance, you might say, "Lord, we're really going through some hard things right now, but I want to thank you for the chance to trust you more, to be a stronger person, and to be the more generous friend to my spouse that I need to be through this challenge we're facing. I am grateful for your trust in me."

Reflection Questions

- Have you ever praised God for your spouse or your marriage, even when you didn't feel like it?
- When do you find it hardest to be grateful in your marriage? How could you make an authentic "sacrifice of praise" in these situations?

Step Two: Approach with Wonder

Keep in mind that praying for your spouse is not about trying to make them into your image and likeness. As tempting as it may be to pray that your husband or wife become as awesome and perfect in every way as you are, that's not going to get you very far.

We tend to treat intercessory prayer as the spiritual equivalent of inserting our debit card into a vending machine. Have a complaint about your marriage? Choose your desired result, swipe your card (by praying really hard), and get the answer you want. But if you don't get the answer you want, one of the dangers is that you might become annoyed with God for "holding out" on you.

And then there is the other extreme. Some spouses feel selfish asking for anything in their marriage. When these very sincere people pray for their relationship, they tend to do so only for the grace to put up with and faithfully endure the latest frustration their spouse has caused them. The prayer is certainly heartfelt—and there is a lot to be said for asking God to help us be more patient with each other—but intercessory prayer is ordered to both forbearance and transformation. It's not wrong to ask God to change your spouse's heart, as well as your own, and to pray that your marriage become better than what it is.

Both approaches—treating prayer like a vending machine and failing to ask God to change situations in your marriage—are manifestations of the same problem: the assertion, in prayer, of our own understanding of marriage over God's intention for marriage as revealed through the Church.

Spouses who take the vending-machine approach assume they have it all figured out when they pray that their mate will change to suit them—and then get annoyed when God doesn't make it happen fast enough (or at all). These husbands and wives may indeed want very good things that would be very good for the marriage. But even if the things we want are good, this posture toward prayer is all wrong. It reveals a fundamental misunderstanding of Christian discipleship and prayer.

Imagine your child lifting his dinner plate and screaming, "Give me an extra helping of broccoli *now*!" Even though your child is asking for something that is good for him, you'd be loath to give it to him. You might want to, and you might be pleased that he wants something healthy, but you know that you'd be creating a monster if you rewarded this way of making a request.

We don't want our relationship with God to turn us into demanding children. Further, he knows what is best for us and for our marriage. On the other hand, he might even answer such a prayer—God, in his generosity, may decide to pick his battles with you, giving you the broccoli now and addressing your approach to prayer in some other way. Still, an approach to prayer that asserts our will over God's can become an obstacle to grace.

Reflection Question

- When are you most tempted to pray that God would make your spouse into your own image and likeness?

It is just as destructive for spouses to pray for nothing more than the ability to put up with the latest challenge they face. This might seem like a humbler approach to prayer than the vending-machine approach, but spouses who pray the help-me-put-up-with-it prayer are not stopping to consider, "What does *God* want to make of my marriage?" They certainly mean well, but they are tempted perhaps by sloth.

As Greg discusses in his book *Broken Gods: Hope, Healing, and the Seven Longings of the Human Heart*, sloth is not the sin of laziness. It is the sin of wiggling out of God's call that we work for justice. In marriage, sloth results when we stare in the face an offense against the dignity of our marriage or ourselves and refuse to engage, not because we are being prudent, but because "(sigh) that's just the way it is (sigh)." Sloth is the sin of embracing a false martyrdom and with it the sick sense of self-righteousness that comes from treating our so-called defective spouse as our "cross." It's putting up with some offensive or destructive behavior rather than standing against it, because "what's the point?" There is a reason so many horrible marriages don't improve when one spouse prays this way, and it isn't necessarily because God refuses to respond to the prayer. Most often it is because God is giving the spouse the grace to deal with the problem directly, but the husband or wife is too busy saying, "Let's not rock the boat, OK?"

Reflection Question

- What problems in your marriage do you tend to ignore or put up with (or ask God to help you ignore or put up with) because "that's just the way it is"?

None of this is meant to be a judgment against anyone who has fallen into these traps. Who among us hasn't tried to pray someone into being more like us or at least more as we want them to be? Who hasn't kept silent when they should have spoken up, or stayed still when they should have acted? We all fail, all the time. But thanks be to God, his mercy is wider than our failures.

That doesn't mean we can't aim higher in our efforts to cooperate with God's grace. We can start by praying with a humble heart that is not afraid to wonder at the great things God wants to do in our life and in our relationship:

"Lord, teach me what *you* want to make of my marriage. Teach me how to be the lover, the partner, and the friend my spouse needs me to be. Give me the grace to challenge my spouse when necessary and to be a blessing and sign of your love, so that your will can be done in our home and we can become everything you created us to be." Praying for our marriage with humility and a sense of childlike wonder opens us to hearing and following God's direction, as he works in and through us for the greater good of our marriage, our children, and the people affected by our marriage.

Imagine your child coming to you and saying, "Please teach me, Mommy. I want to learn this." Or, "Daddy, I don't know how to do this, but I know *you* can show me. Will you? Please?" What parent would refuse such a request? If we who are evil can give good things to our children, how much more will our Father in heaven give good things to us (see Matthew 7:11)?

When you pray for your marriage, begin by recognizing that you *don't* know the answer to many situations you face or how to direct those situations so that they yield the best outcome. In fact, you are praying to know God's will. The only thing you know for sure is that God wants to make you and your spouse saints, that he wants to give you a love that satisfies the deepest longings of your hearts, and that he wants your marriage to be a light to those you encounter. Of course, you have no idea how he is going to pull *that* off, so you are here to learn. Approaching God with a sense of wonder, a genuine openness to his grace, and a willingness to go where he leads is the key to fruitful marital intercession.

Anytime you pray for your marriage, begin by forthrightly describing what is going on—good, bad, or otherwise—and saying, "Please, Lord, give us the grace to be the couple you want us to be as we receive this blessing (or confront this trial). Help me to be the spouse that my mate needs me to be in the face of this. And help my spouse be open to your grace that comes through our marriage and flows through each of us."

Do you want your wife to handle her work stress better? "Please, Lord, give me the grace to really be in this situation with my wife. Help me be the husband my wife needs me to be, in order to support her and encourage her through the stress of it all. Help my wife see how much I am trying to be here for her, and let your grace flow through my heart to hers."

Do you want your husband to be a more prayerful man? "Lord God, bless my husband. Help us be the faithful, prayerful couple you want us to be. Help me not be afraid to share my faith with him, even when he rolls his eyes at me. Help me always have the courage to live for you in this marriage, and help my husband be open to the grace you want to give him through me."

Do you want your spouse to be more passionate, attentive, understanding, levelheaded, patient, communicative—you name it? "Lord, help my spouse with X. Help us to be the couple you want us to be. Give me the grace to support, encourage, and challenge my spouse to grow in X, especially when I feel confused, or unsure, or even a little scared. Help my spouse be open to the things you are asking me to do, so that we can both grow in the ways that would help us be everything you want us to be."

Do you see? Use your own words, of course, but whatever words you use and whether you employ more formal prayer or a more conversational approach, always pray for your marriage and your spouse with that sense of childlike wonder, confidence, and hope that comes from being willing to learn what your heavenly Father wants to teach you about his plan for your lives together.

Reflection Question

- What would change about the way you pray for your marriage if you asked God to teach you instead of telling God what he can do for you?

Step Three: Pray, "Lord, Change Me!"

The third step in praying for your spouse is to ask God to change *you*.

But . . . but . . . ! We know. How does praying that God change you constitute praying for your spouse? Well, consider the fact that you are meant to be an instrument of grace in your marriage. By all means, with your first breath, pray that your spouse would be healthy, strong, faithful, compassionate, understanding, gentle, wise, passionate, and all the rest. But with your next breath, make sure you pray, "And help me be the spouse my mate needs me to become."

Prayer isn't magic. It is grace in action. Pope Francis once said, "You pray for the hungry. Then you feed them. That's how prayer works!" In the same way, you must pray that God would give you the grace to be the encourager your spouse needs you to be, or the support, or the catalyst for the change you want to see in your spouse, or whatever else is on the agenda. That's how praying for your spouse works!

We don't mean to suggest that God cannot or will not move in any way other than through you. God is not limited by anything! He is God, after all. "Anything is possible" is literally part of his job description (see Luke 1:37).

That said, God created a certain order in the world, and for the most part, because he loves the world he created, he tends to work in ways that respect that order. Miracles happen, but they are not the norm. That's what makes them miracles! If God wants to work a miracle in your marriage by circumventing you and providing directly for your spouse, great! Be open to that. In the meantime, ask God to make you who he needs you to be so that he can bless your spouse through you.

Step Four: Listen

But *how* does God want you to change? Does he want you to suck it up if you're unhappy? Does he want you to fight every battle to the nth degree? How do you know what God wants?

You listen! In prayer, you quiet your mind and your spirit and open your heart to let God speak deep within. How do you listen? What are you listening for?

St. Ignatius of Loyola, a master of discernment, considered three major ways God speaks. First, sometimes he speaks in unmistakable ways that let us know *God is talking now. Listen up!* When this happens, it is usually accompanied by an overwhelming sense that "I *must* do this!" accompanied by the recognition that we should give our consent and get out of God's way. God rarely speaks to us like this, but it does happen, and it is almost always life changing when it does.

Reflection Questions

- When has God revealed himself to you in some dramatic way?
- Has he ever revealed his will this way in your marriage?

The second way God speaks to us is quieter. We pray. We observe. We take our observations to prayer. And little by little, a sense grows within us that *this* is the right choice to make. Usually this mode of communication serves us best when we are torn between two possible good choices. Clarity comes slowly but unmistakably, like the breaking dawn.

Reflection Questions

- When has God revealed himself to you as you slowly reflected upon your situation in prayer?
- Has he ever revealed his will this way in your marriage?

The third and most common way God speaks to us is through our reason, our God-given ability to think things through and choose what is good. People often discount this, saying, "How do I know it's really God talking and not just me?" But if we are drawn toward a good and godly thing, then God is talking to us, even if we need help from others to discern exactly what we need to do.

God is the author and giver of our reason. If we think good thoughts and desire things that would truly be good for us and for the people we love, God is in it in some way. As St. Augustine is famously paraphrased, "Love God and do as you please: for the soul trained in love to God will do nothing to offend the One who is Beloved."[7] It is never "just us" motivating us to do good things or pursue good goals. It is always the love of God within us propelling us forward, whether or not we realize it.

God draws us toward three qualities as we listen for his voice: meaningfulness, intimacy, and virtue. *Meaningfulness* is a way to describe our commitment to use the gifts God has given us—our talents and abilities—to do whatever we reasonably can to help others become their best selves. When we see ourselves making a positive difference—not tearing people down or simply leaving them as we found them—we experience our lives as meaningful. As the Church teaches, we find ourselves only in making a sincere gift of ourselves.[8]

Reflection Questions

- How are you using your gifts to help your spouse become the person he or she is meant to be?
- How might focusing on God's call to meaningfulness change the way you approach future decisions that affect your marriage?

Intimacy refers to the commitment to always do what we reasonably can to make our relationships healthier, deeper, stronger, godlier, closer. Sometimes, when we are with people who are safe and godly, it means opening up more than we care to. Other times, when we are with people who would use us or attempt to undermine our God-given dignity, we are called to impose boundaries that trim the relationship back to a healthier place. Either way, God is always calling us to communion and, in the context of this book, to communion here and now with our spouse. Recall that in the beginning, when mankind was first created, God said, "It is not good for the man to be alone" (Genesis 2:18).

Reflection Questions

- When was the last time you shared a little bit more of yourself with your spouse or set a boundary with your spouse that made the relationship stronger, healthier, or closer?

- How would focusing on God's call to deeper intimacy change the way you make future decisions that affect your marriage?

Finally, *virtue* refers to the decision to see life as a series of opportunities to make choices that enable us to grow into our best selves. To consistently ask, "How can I use *this* situation, *this* moment, *this* interaction, to grow closer to being the whole, healed, godly, and grace-filled person I am meant to be?" Doing this means more than being nice or not rocking the boat or not fighting back. It means looking for the ways I can use this present moment to become a little bit better than I am, so that in my marriage, I can be all that I am meant to be.

Reflection Questions

- How have your decisions in your marriage helped you be more of the whole, healed, godly, grace-filled person God created you to be?
- How might meditating on meaningfulness, intimacy, and virtue affect the way you approach decision making in the future?

In every situation, we can prayerfully ask, "What is the most meaningful, intimate, and virtuous response I can reasonably make to the person or situation in front of me?" If we do this, we will tune the antennae of our reason to the grace-filled signal God is broadcasting and hear him quietly speaking to us in even the most mundane moments of married life.

Step Five: Repeat

Remember, prayer is ultimately about union with God. We pray about the concerns of our life and marriage, and God hears those prayers and attends to those concerns in his way and in his time. But all the while, God is using the process of our prayer to draw us into deeper union with him. In order for prayer to do its thing, so to speak, we need to keep praying, especially when it seems pointless, when we feel as if God isn't listening and the answer isn't forthcoming.

If you are concerned about your marriage or your household, it's important to bring your cares to the Lord, who is waiting, always, to hear the cry of your heart. There are a million other problems in the world you aren't focusing on right now. Why are you focusing on *this* concern so much? God wants to meet you in this need. Keep coming back to him with an open heart and expectant faith.

In the movie *The Karate Kid*, a young man wants to learn the art of self-defense. The karate master orders the young student to perform an endless series of menial tasks. This goes on for weeks. Eventually frustrated, the boy rebels and demands that his lessons finally start. The master attacks him, punching and kicking as he yells out the names of the chores he has asked the boy to do. The boy reflexively adopts the body positions involved in the chores and is shocked to discover that he blocks every one of the master's attacks. For weeks the boy thought he was waxing the master's car, mopping his floor, and doing a hundred other household tasks. But all the while, he was learning the art of self-defense. He was focusing on one thing, but the master was teaching him something else entirely.

Prayer is like that. We ask for help paying this unexpected bill, and the Lord honors that prayer in some way. Then we ask for help getting through this argument with our mate, and he honors that in some way. And then we come to him about some other worldly concern, and another, and another; and regardless of what we ask him, regardless of what mundane, menial concerns we are preoccupied with, God uses those prayers about earthly things to teach us the heavenly art of becoming the man or woman we were meant to be as we draw closer to him. With prayer there is always a lot more going on than meets the eye, and as we stick with the process, we will find that we learn whatever the master is trying to teach us.

That's why, when we pray, we stay with it and keep coming back to God over and over—not because God is deaf, but because we are. Don't ever say, "I prayed about that marriage situation or family problem, so I don't need to mention it again." Or, "I prayed about this household situation, and God didn't answer me." As long as the situation remains an issue, he is asking you to keep coming back to him in prayer, so that he can teach you the next "moves."

Make sure you ask him to open your heart to his lessons. "Lord, I really need help with this [household issue or marriage struggle or parenting problem]. Please show me and my spouse what to do. And please help us be open to what you are trying to say to us while you lead us through this. Make us the people you need us to be in the face of this challenge, and help us to stay even closer to you—and each other—while we walk through this together."

Reflection Questions

- In what ways have you grown closer to God through your marriage?
- How might your approach to prayer change if you could be aware of the ways God is asking you to grow and draw closer to him through all the concerns you bring to his attention?

When you intercede for your spouse and your marriage in the manner outlined in this chapter, whatever prayer forms you use, you are opening yourself to God so that he can pour his grace into your life and your home. All the little blessings, mundane tasks, and even challenging problems you face help you become the whole, healed, godly, and grace-filled couple you were meant to be. They are preparing you to one day celebrate—together—the eternal wedding feast of heaven.

CHAPTER FOUR

Praying with Your Spouse: Why and How to Do It . . . Painlessly

According to a 2014 survey by Georgetown's Center for Applied Research in the Apostolate, commissioned by Holy Cross Family Ministries, only 17 percent of Catholic couples pray together. You might think that figure applies to things like the Rosary or more lengthy forms of prayer, but unfortunately, according to the study, only 13 percent of Catholic families even manage to say grace before meals together.

Think about this. Did you know that saying grace slowly, in a thoughtful manner, literally takes eight seconds? Don't believe us? Go ahead. Time it. We'll wait.

Bless us, O Lord, and these thy gifts, which we are about to receive through thy bounty through Christ our Lord. Amen.

Eight seconds. See? Told ya.

The point of this little exercise is to illustrate the lie we all tell ourselves. "Oh, gosh, we *wish* we could pray together, but we're so busy. Where would we find the time?" In truth, today's couples are so busy they don't have time *not* to pray! The real issue is that most of us simply don't think about praying as a couple.

It's understandable, of course. Many of us were not raised in homes where our families prayed together, so we don't have a model for how to do it. Prayer seems strange, alien, and maybe even a little scary.

Isn't Prayer Private?

When we talk about praying as a couple, someone inevitably asks, "But isn't prayer supposed to be private?"

The Church does encourage us to pray daily, and a portion of this prayer is usually one-on-one with the Lord. In other words, it is private in the commonly understood sense of "apart from others." But all prayer, whether alone or with others, has a public dimension.

As the *Catechism* says, "Prayer is *Christian* insofar as it is communion with Christ and extends throughout the Church, which is his Body" (2565). Christian prayer may be personal, it is certainly intimate, and it can be performed privately. But by its nature, it is communal, because its effects always extend beyond the individual who is praying.

In a fundamental way, then, your prayer time, both individual and as a couple, is never private. It always takes place within the heart of the Church, in union with the angels and saints, and flows out to your marriage, your family, your friends and acquaintances, the Church, and the world. So if you're resisting the notion of praying as a couple by insisting that prayer is private, get over that hump now. Prayer never takes place in isolation.

The bottom line is that praying together as a couple will help you have a vibrant Christian marriage. Why? Because if a husband and wife are going to fulfill the spiritual mission of their marriage, they have to share a spiritual life. How else are they going to raise children, serve the poor, care for the lonely, visit the sick and the elderly, and do similar works of discipleship *as a couple* across a lifetime together?

Let's be clear. We don't mean to suggest that God is not present in the home of a husband and wife who do not pray together, or that you should feel ashamed of yourself if you haven't prayed together before. Both things would be absurd—if not outright offensive—to suggest! After all, God is always present, bidden or unbidden, and the invitation to pray as a couple is meant to be just that, an *invitation* to celebrate your marriage on a deeper, more loving, more intimate, more joyful level. Such an invitation is cause for joy, not shame.

A husband and wife could very well have a perfectly pleasant, functional marriage even without praying together. But failing to pray together—especially in a sacramental marriage—is akin to cutting off one of your legs (or allowing your spouse to do it). Could you learn to live a satisfying life even in the face of such a tragedy? Of course. But given the choice, would you rather be able to walk on both legs? Of course.

With or without couple prayer, the degree of satisfaction you have achieved in your relationship is something to be celebrated. But regardless of whether your marriage is currently deeply satisfying or is experiencing serious challenges, prayer together will take your marriage to a deeper lever, a more joyful level, and a spiritual level that few couples think is possible much less dream about. Your marriage—whether good or challenging—cannot help but be better if you pray together as a couple.

In fact, a recent study by the University of Texas found that when couples agreed that they (1) had a God-centered marriage; (2) shared core spiritual values; and (3) regularly engaged in shared religious practices (prayer, Bible reading, and so forth) outside of church *during* the week, they reported more stability and satisfaction in their relationship.

Praying together as a couple is both good and good for you! Whatever your feelings about this might be, we hope to convince you to stick your toe in the water. We're confident that once you do, and if you stay with it, you'll be amazed at the difference it makes in the closeness you feel, the strength of your communication, and even your ability to express your passion for each other more freely.

Regarding that last point, research has shown that couples who pray together have more satisfying sex lives. The authors of the study noted that couples who prayed together said that they were able to relate on more levels, which made every aspect of their relationship more enjoyable, including sex.

Prayer Rules

We understand that you might still be a little nervous, even if you have decided to give it a go. But whether you are new to praying together or old hands, let's take a moment to review some basic rules that will make your experience feel comfortable, safe, and meaningful.

There isn't one right way to pray together.

Sometimes, as a couple first begins to pray together, the entire process breaks down over arguments about the "best" or "right" way to do it. There are certainly *different* ways to pray, but different is not the same as right or best. The only qualifier is that prayer needs to come from the heart. Even the simplest prayer—formal or informal, traditional or unconventional—is prayer if it comes from your heart.

Make it a habit. Assuming you are both bringing your hearts to the process, you have to do it regularly, regardless of what specific form it takes. You can always work to make it more rewarding or meaningful down the line, but there is no chance of going deeper in your prayer time if it isn't happening in the first place.

How long? Pray for the length of time that is most manageable. That will vary according to your current circumstances. Your goal is to have a personally meaningful experience of God that draws you closer to each other as well. Even taking the time to pray a thoughtful Glory Be can be a good beginning if it happens consistently and is said from the heart.

Make a plan. Pick a time that works best for you, preferably a time when you are together anyway. You are more likely to make prayer time happen if you do it in bed when you first wake up, for example, or immediately after dinner, or perhaps when you go to bed together at night. These are just suggestions. The point is, try to make your prayer a natural part of the times when you are already together, rather than choosing some random time when one of you has to track the other down because "we're supposed to have prayer time now."

Reflection Questions

- What are some of your favorite ways to pray? How could you adapt these so that you and your spouse could use them as you pray together?
- When do you think it would be most natural for you and your spouse to have a regular and meaningful prayer time? Why would this time work best for you?

Expect to grow.

Begin where you are comfortable, and challenge each other to grow from there. A year from now, if you are praying in exactly the same way you pray today—, not putting anything more into it or getting anything more out of it—then something is decidedly wrong. That's not to say you have to constantly experiment with different types of prayer in order to do it "right." After all, as we've established, as long as you are bringing your heart to it, there isn't one right way to pray together. But your prayer ought to evolve the more you do it, because prayer is about a relationship with God and each other.

If you got together with the same person every week, for example, and always said the same things and did the same things, you wouldn't have much of a relationship. For the friendship to grow, it needs to develop and put down roots over time. The same is true of prayer.

As a couple, you might stick to certain types of prayer that you enjoy more. That's fine, but remember to bring more of yourself to the process as time goes by. If you begin with formal or traditional prayers, like the Glory Be or Our Father, for example, a next step might be adding a few words of praise and thanksgiving or your prayer intentions for the day. If you say a Rosary together, you might try meditative versions that use brief scriptural reflections for each decade, allowing you to enter more deeply into prayer. If, on the other hand, you prefer spontaneous prayer, you might experiment with more structure by integrating some traditional prayers of the Church into your prayer time or doing *lectio divina* together.

The point is, once you have established a regular prayer ritual as a couple, you want to avoid the trap of thinking of prayer as something you do rather than as a relationship that you are developing with God and your spouse. Relationships involve more than going through the motions and checking off the boxes. You need to think about them and plan what you are going to bring to the table—emotionally and spiritually—the next time you are with that person. Prayer is no different.

For your prayer life to evolve, you need to think about it and reflect on it even when you aren't praying. In fact, if you recall, this is an important dimension of the listening part of prayer. Think about what you want to pray about as you go through your day. Make a mental note to bring these blessings or intentions to your prayer time with your spouse.

Reflection Questions

- What do you think it would mean to "go a little deeper" in your prayer life? What would it be like for you to share a deeper prayer life with your spouse?
- Review the different types of prayer we described in chapter 2. Which types are unfamiliar to you? What would it be like for you and your spouse to explore those types of prayer together?

Don't criticize. Encourage.

We're all human. Sometimes we have little enthusiasm to do anything, even something as wonderful as spending time with God or our spouse. Other times we get a little lazy and just phone in our prayers, so to speak, saying the words without giving much thought to the meaning behind them.

That's OK. God still likes spending time with us, even if we're a little distracted occasionally. But sometimes our distraction can devolve into laziness and become habitual. When that happens, one or the other of you will need to step up and address the situation. It goes without saying that you should never criticize each other's prayer, but it can be a good thing to encourage each other to be a little more present, a little more honest, and a little more authentic in your prayer as time goes by.

Here's what the difference between criticism and encouragement looks like in practice.

Imagine that you have been having a regular prayer time, but you feel that your spouse has become somewhat grudging about praying together and seems to be distracted while doing it.

Criticism: Why should we even bother trying to pray together if you're not going to try?

Encouragement: Honey, I appreciate your making time to pray together, but you haven't really seemed all here for a while. What can we do to make this more meaningful for you? Is there something that's distracting you? Could we pray about it?

See the difference? The critical approach is hostile and judgmental and likely to provoke a defensive response: "What do you mean? I'm praying! Why don't *you* stop staring at me and try focusing more on God yourself?!"

By contrast, the encouraging approach brings your concern into the open but invites your spouse to actually pray about whatever the problem is. Perhaps your spouse is feeling disconnected from God or is upset about unanswered prayer. Perhaps there is some other problem, and it hasn't occurred to either of you that it's OK to pray about it. (It happens to all of us.) Bringing these concerns into the open and attaching an invitation to pray about them, whatever they are, allow you to use the resistance as an opportunity to grow closer to God and each other.

Let's try another example. Imagine that you are a husband who is frustrated because your wife seems intent on sticking with only one kind of prayer and is having a hard time stepping outside her spiritual comfort zone.

Criticism: There you go again. Why does it always have to be the same thing?
Encouragement: I know how much praying X way means to you. This time I'd really like to do Y. If you'd still like to do X after, that would be OK with me, but let's try this for the next week and see how it goes.

In this example, the critical approach is not only hostile and personal, it's also passive and powerless. Your spouse will most likely respond antagonistically, and you will feel stuck and frustrated.

The encouraging approach is simultaneously more sensitive and more assertive. You are respecting what is important to your spouse while asserting what is important to you. You aren't asking your spouse to give up anything, only to try something else as well.

Understanding the difference between criticism and encouragement—in general but especially in your prayer life—allows you to foster a deeper spirit of prayer and avoids any implication that you are grading your spouse's performance.

Don't ask permission.

This tip is probably going to raise some eyebrows, but hear us out.

There are certain things that are normal parts of a healthy relationship, and you shouldn't ever feel obliged to ask permission to do them. For instance, you would never go to your spouse and say, "Is it OK to eat today?" Or, "What do you think? Should we ever pay our bills again?" Or, "I know we prefer ignoring each other, but is it OK if we tried to have a conversation today?"

These things are essential to a healthy life and relationship—you don't need anyone's permission to do them. For the Christian couple, prayer is one of these things. You don't need to ask permission to pray with your spouse, nor do you need to apologize for wanting to pray with your spouse. It is as normal and necessary a part of Christian marriage as eating together, communicating, or any other common relationship activity.

In fact, if your spouse tried to prevent you from eating or paying the bills, or if he or she actively resisted any kind of meaningful conversation, you would see that as a serious problem that warranted professional attention. A spouse who absolutely refuses to pray with you is inflicting a similar kind of injury on you and your marriage. They deny you the right to exercise a basic function of Christian marriage

That said, while you should never feel the need to ask permission to pray with your spouse, you have no right to be a spiritual bully either. As if you could win anyone's heart that way. Can you imagine? "We're going to pray now, dammit, and you're going to like it!" Probably not the best way to go about your spiritual life as a couple.

So what can you do? If there is something that needs to be prayed about, be confident in taking the lead in praying about it, even if prayer isn't your spouse's thing. Are you and your spouse facing a big decision, for example? Somewhere in the middle of the conversation, especially if one or both of you is feeling stuck, just say, "I feel like this is something we need to bring to God." *And then jump right in:* "Lord, please bless us and help us make the decision that glorifies you and builds up your kingdom."

Don't make a question out of whether or not to pray. Definitely don't make it an attack. Just make it something you do because it is important, and it wouldn't occur to you not to do it.

Compare this with a more permission-seeking, apologetic approach.

Wife: "Would it be OK if we took some time to pray about this?"
Husband: "Uh, I guess." (Rolls eyes.)
Wife: "Fine. If you don't want to, never mind."

Here's another example. Are you and your spouse arguing? That's a great time to just stop and say, "I feel like we could both use God's help right now. 'Lord, we're really having a tough time working through our frustrations with each other. Please help us figure this out and be loving to each other as we work through it.'"

Compare this to the more permission-seeking, apologetic alternative.

> Wife: I really wish you would just pray with me already!
> Husband: You knew I wasn't like that when we got married! Why are you trying to change me?
> Wife: I'm not trying to change you. I just want to pray about this instead of fighting,
> Husband: Well, I don't.
> Wife: Fine.

Taking the direct approach allows you to affirm the rightness, naturalness, and appropriateness of praying together, while avoiding—for the most part—the passive aggression, resentment, and powerlessness that come from the permission-seeking, apologetic approach.

Reflection Questions

- When do I tend to be more critical than encouraging in my marriage? What might I do to approach these situations in a more encouraging way in the future?
- In what ways could I do a better job encouraging my spouse's spiritual growth?

- Are there times I get discouraged in our attempts at prayer? How might I approach these situations in a more productive way?

Address the real problem.

This is usually the point at which someone will say, "But my wife isn't Christian," or, "My husband gets angry if I try to pray with him. I can't make him love God, so isn't it better just to leave it alone?"

No. It's not. And here's why. At its root, conflict about praying together isn't simply religious disagreement. It is a failure of respect.

As Greg points out in *How to Heal Your Marriage and Nurture Lasting Love,* couples in a healthy marriage don't always like the same things or think and feel the same ways about everything. But if a couple is healthy, they don't ignore each other—the wife, for example, letting her husband do his own thing as long as she is allowed to stay out of it. They *respect* each other enough to try to find the truth, goodness, and beauty in all the things their spouse finds true, good, and beautiful.

That is what true respect involves. Respecting your spouse means that if something is important to your partner, then there is something important about it, and it deserves your support. Assuming your spouse is not drawn to something that is immoral, demeaning, or contrary to the wellbeing of the marriage, basic respect dictates that you find it in your heart not only to tolerate that thing but to actively support your spouse's involvement—including being as involved in that activity as you reasonably can, even if it isn't your thing.

There are many couples who aren't in the same place spiritually. But this is only a problem when there is a failure of basic respect in the marriage. When couples respect each other, and one spouse wishes to pray as a couple, the other spouse at least tries to participate. That could involve anything from joining in whatever kinds of prayer they are comfortable with, to maintaining a thoughtful and attentive silence while their spouse prays, to having conversations about the prayer afterward, even though they weren't exactly sure how to participate during the prayer.

Respectful spouses are naturally inclined to see the truth, goodness, and beauty in whatever the other finds true, good, and beautiful. This is the case even when they don't understand it and even if it is outside their comfort zone. Granted, this requires a certain level of maturity but one no greater than the maturity marriage demands of any spouse.

If your spouse consistently groans about praying together—not in a "This isn't really my thing, but if it's that important to you, I'm willing to come along the best I can" sort of way, but in a "There is no way you are ever going to make me do this, and I will make you miserable if you try" sort of way—then you do not have a religious problem in your marriage. You have a marriage problem that is playing itself out over religion and probably plays itself out in other areas as well.

Consider other areas of your relationship besides religion and prayer. What is your spouse's response when something is more important or interesting to you than to them? Does he fight you? Is she resentful? Does he merely tolerate your involvement but have almost zero interest in sharing those things with you? Does she get involved but "punish" you by dragging her feet and pouting the whole time? Does this happen with things that have nothing to do with religion, perhaps involving your family, or parenting style, or finances, or sexuality, or interests and hobbies? The degree to which you see this resistance being played out in these areas, as well as in prayer together, is the degree to which you have a respect issue rather than a religious one.

So what do you do if this is the case? You seek professional help. If you don't have your spouse's respect, you will not be able to make any changes in your marriage—spiritual or otherwise. A husband who fails to respect his wife or a wife who fails to respect her husband will feel no obligation to listen when the needs, interests, or desires of their partner conflict with theirs.

The first step in addressing this issue is reframing it. When your spouse resists prayer, say, "I understand that I'm asking you to do something that makes you uncomfortable, but I would never think of asking you to do this with me if I didn't believe it was absolutely essential for a healthy marriage. I promise I will be sensitive and try to make this as workable for you as possible, but I need you to try to see this through my eyes and do it with me to whatever degree you are able. Can you do that for me?"

A mature and respectful spouse will never say no to this. He or she might struggle a bit and ask tough questions, but that's good! That's the beginning of an authentic spiritual life.

An immature spouse who is not respectful, on the other hand, will respond by pouting, throwing a tantrum, lecturing, or undermining your efforts at every turn, up to and including trying to make you feel guilty for "cheating" on them with God or putting your faith before your marriage. The problem is, for the Christian, faith must come before anything else. Otherwise you create a false god out of your spouse by placing their desires over your responsibility to consecrate your marriage, family, and home to Christ.

It is beyond the scope of this book to walk you through the steps to heal this problem. We address the issue more thoroughly in both *How to Heal Your Marriage and Nurture Lasting Love* and *Discovering God Together: The Catholic Guide to Raising Faithful Kids*. Additionally, we work with many couples who struggle with this issue through the Pastoral Solutions Institute's telephone counseling practice.[9]

The takeaway is that you should never believe that you are doing something wrong when you invite your spouse to join you in prayer to whatever degree they are able. Yes, you will need to be sensitive. Yes, you will need to be supportive. Yes, you will need to be patient, understanding, loving, encouraging, and grateful for their willingness to extend themselves out of respect for you and your faith. But this is nothing less than one spouse is expected to do for another.

Reflection Questions

- Do I feel respected by my spouse, especially in my spiritual desires for our marriage, family, and home life?
- What steps could I take to be more respectful in regard to the things that are important to my spouse?
- How can I become more confident about inviting my spouse to pray with me? What would be different about my approach to prayer if I could have this confidence?

Ask God to teach you.

Finally, when you pray together, dedicate at least part of your prayer time to asking God to help you be the couple he wants you to be. Ask God to teach you to love each other, not only with your human love, but with the love that comes from his own heart. Dedicate your marriage to him each day. Ask him to give you the grace you need to glorify him in the way you manage conflict; handle problems; make decisions; prioritize each other's needs, desires, and concerns; and, most importantly, show your love for each other.

Ask God to bless your marriage in every way possible, and expect to be amazed by the ways God uses your human love to raise you to new heights of passion, joy, and holiness.

Reflection Questions

- How might my spouse and I become better at showing God's love to each other?
- What would change about my approach to marriage if my spouse and I were to dedicate our marriage to God every day?

An Invitation

We hope that by using some of the tips in this chapter, you and your spouse will come to celebrate a mature, respectful, meaningful, and rewarding experience of prayer together. Sometimes this comes easily; other times it will be a challenge. But whatever you face along the way, committing to the journey of prayer together will allow you to experience God's love in new ways, inspire you to draw from God's love to better love each other, and empower you to be a real witness in the world of the amazing things God can do in the lives of those who love him and seek him together.

Part Two

Praying Your Way through Your Marriage

CHAPTER FIVE

Praying for Your Daily Life

W hether you are praying for your marriage on your own or praying with your spouse, the most common springboard for your prayer life will be the daily blessings, challenges, and decisions you face as a couple. In this chapter, we'll look at different, simple ways you can approach your day as a husband or wife more prayerfully, bringing God with you throughout your day and inviting him into every part of your relationship. We hope that these suggestions will inspire you to deepen and expand upon the ways you currently pray for and with your spouse.

Good Morning!

> *In the morning I will sing of your love;*
> *for you are my fortress, my refuge in times of trouble.*
> *(Psalm 59:16, NIV)*

Every day is a gift from God. How should we respond to this gift as a spouse or a couple?

Imagine giving your children a gift that "requires some assembly." What is the first thing your kids do after they unwrap their present and jump up and down in excitement? They ask you to help them put it together, of course!

We think this example has something to say about how we might respond to the gift of each day. As we wake up, we unwrap the gift of the new day. Regardless of how we feel about the things we will face in the coming hours, we run to the arms of our heavenly Father and ask for his help in assembling this new day according to his purpose.

It's tempting to behave instead like a toddler and run away with our new day, screaming, "*Do by self! Do by self! Do by self!*" But this turns out about as well as allowing a toddler to make all the arrangements for our day. Better to bring our life and marriage, our hopes and dreams, our fears and struggles, and all the rest to God in the very first moments of the day.

Traditionally Catholics have done this by means of the prayer known as the Morning Offering. The most common version of this prayer—used by individuals all over the world—is

> *O Jesus, through the Immaculate Heart of Mary, I offer you my prayers, works, joys, and sufferings of this day for all the intentions of your Sacred Heart, in union with the Holy Sacrifice of the Mass throughout the world, for the salvation of souls, the reparation for sins, the reunion of all Christians, and in particular for the intentions of the Holy Father this month. Amen.*[10]

If you wanted to stick to the classics, such as this Morning Offering, but still specifically mention your marriage and family life, you could add to the second line, "I offer you my prayers, works, joys, and sufferings of this day, *especially those of my marriage and family life.*" Technically, of course, your marriage and family life are included in this prayer, but we like to add this little reminder that our relationships aren't just incidental to the day.

Giving your marriage and family to God each day upon waking up is a powerful reminder that you are not on your own. God is with you every step of the way. He will strengthen you, encourage you, bless you, and challenge you to use every thought, word, and act of the day to bless the people in your life and to build his kingdom. What a fantastic reminder of the wonderful things God wants to do with your marriage!

Calling this version of the Morning Offering a classic is a bit misleading, since Christianity is more than two thousand years old, and this particular version of the prayer wasn't written until 1844. Obviously, Christians were praising God at the beginning of the day in their own ways and their own words for quite some time before Fr. François-Xavier Gautrelet put pen to paper and composed it. You should also feel free to bring your day to God in whatever way you and your spouse see fit.

For example, in addition to the Morning Offering, we often take turns saying some variation on the following when we first wake up, before we even get out of bed:

Lord, thank you for this new day. Thank you for each other and for letting us share another day together. Please help us be the husband and wife for each other that we each need, that you want us to be. Help us love each other generously, passionately, and gracefully, so that we can see your love for us shining out through one another. Be with us as we face the challenges of the day [you might mention some petitions here]. Give us individually and together all the strength we need to overcome these challenges and the eyes to see you blessing us through it all. Lord, let us glorify you in everything we do. Help us be a couple after your own heart, so you can use us to be a sign of your love to each other and the world. Amen.

You get the idea. Sometimes we'll add a decade of the Rosary, or a whole Rosary if there's time, or perhaps a Chaplet of Divine Mercy, the short prayer from St. Faustina that uses the beads of the rosary to reflect on the merciful love of God.

A morning offering prayer, in whatever way you do it, brings your life and marriage to God, helping you rejoice in the gifts that you have been given and opening your hearts to God's presence with you and his will for you each day. This beautiful habit has brought countless blessings to our relationship, reminding us to be truly grateful for each other (especially when we don't feel like it), encouraging us to be loving to each other (especially when we don't feel like it), and challenging us to help each other become the people God wants us to be (especially when we don't feel like it).

Reflection Questions

- Do you currently have a way to give each day to God? Do you share this with your spouse? Would there be a simple way to adapt what you already do to include your mate?
- Did the suggestions in this section inspire you to think of other ways you and your spouse could bring your marriage and your day to God?

The Liturgy of the Hours

The Divine Office, also known as the Liturgy of the Hours, offers another meaningful way to pray as a couple, not only in the morning but throughout the day.

The Liturgy of the Hours is a standardized series of daily Scripture readings, psalm responses, and petitions that many priests and religious pray daily and all Christians can pray as well. Historically, priests and religious came together in their religious communities at set times throughout the day and into the night to pray the Divine Office and reflect on the word of God. Many religious still pray the full Liturgy of the Hours, but laypeople tend to pray only Morning Prayer and Evening Prayer. If you choose to pray these prayers with your spouse, you can find them on apps and websites specifically devoted to the Divine Office, as well as in books. (Traditionally, the book containing the Divine Office is known as a breviary.)

Praying the Liturgy of the Hours with your spouse is a great way to join your prayers to that of the whole Church, to reflect on Scripture, and to remember that your little domestic church (that is, your marriage and family) is a local outpost of the larger, universal Church. You can personalize this prayer as well with your own petitions and words of praise and thanksgiving, using this more structured prayer as a springboard to deeper communion with God and each other.

Throughout the Day

Don't forget to stay connected to each other throughout the day, especially when spiritual needs arise or blessings happen. Even if you spend many hours apart, as most couples do, you can keep each other posted about the ways God is blessing you and the prayer requests you'd like your spouse to keep in mind.

The other day, for example, Lisa sent Greg a Facebook message, "Got to our appointment just in time. Parking space right up front! Thank you, God!" It was a small note, but it brought a smile to Greg's face, and he typed back, "I'm glad you're there safe. Praying for your meeting!"

This simple exchange—one of many sent back and forth between us throughout the day—allowed us to stay connected even though we were apart most of the day. We appreciate the closeness we gain from these little messages and the opportunities they give us to hold each other in prayer, to rejoice together, and to keep each other updated about the happenings of the day that we will discuss in more detail later on. These little things, when they go unremarked, tend to get lost in the middle of the ten thousand other things that happen.

These prayers of praise, thanksgiving, and intercession are the threads we use to weave the marital, three-ply cord that binds us more tightly to each other and God in good times and bad, sickness and health, wealth and poverty, all the days of our life. A marital prayer life needn't be relegated to certain times during the day. Ideally, it should reflect an ongoing, daily conversation between a husband and wife, in union with God—a conversation that allows them to celebrate the Lord's blessings together and draw spiritual support from God's grace and each other.

Reflection Questions

- Have you ever prayed the Liturgy of the Hours? Did you find this form of prayer helpful? Do you feel led to share this beautiful prayer as a couple? How might you do this?
- Do you and your spouse stay in touch throughout the day? How could this practice of keeping in touch through prayer strengthen your connection to God and each other?

Praying over Each Other

Praying over each other is another simple yet powerful way to integrate prayer into your daily relationship. This can be particularly important when one of you is facing a special challenge, a big opportunity, or physical or emotional upheaval. The power of human touch is well documented for its ability to help slow heart rates, improve restful breathing, and relieve muscle tension. When we lay hands on our spouse in prayer, we combine these physical benefits with the grace that is intended to soothe the body, mind, and soul.

The process is simple. Place one hand on your spouse's head or shoulder, and pray for God's blessing. For instance, if your wife is worried about a job interview, you might place your hand on her shoulder and pray, "Lord, please bless my wife in this interview. Give her your grace, so that she knows the answers to the questions they ask her. Let them see all the wonderful strengths and gifts I see in her. Let her know that I will support her and believe in her no matter what. And let your will be done." Then you might add, "We ask the Blessed Mother's intercession as we pray, Hail Mary . . ."

Likewise, if your husband is struggling with the flu or some other illness, you might lay your hand on him and pray, "Lord, please heal my husband. Give him back his health and strength. Let him know how much I love him, and help me give him the love and care he needs. Archangel Raphael, healing angel of God, pray for us."

This kind of laying on of hands differs from the blessing that a priest gives by virtue of his ordination, a blessing that confers specific graces. But offering a prayer accompanied by the laying on of hands in the manner we suggest is perfectly appropriate to the common priesthood of the faithful as exercised in the domestic church. Through this simple gesture and our simple words, we commit ourselves to supporting our spouse emotionally and physically and commending them and their concerns to God's grace. This laying on of hands in prayer is another example of how the experiences of everyday life can provide opportunities to enter into more intimate conversation with each other and God.

Reflection Questions

- Have you ever prayed over your spouse in the way we describe?
- What would it be like to make a habit of praying over each other in special times of need?

Prayers at Meals

Mealtime is another wonderful opportunity to pray as a couple. If you are blessed to have a meal together, take a moment to thank God for the goodness you have experienced since the last time you sat down together. Then ask his blessings for the challenges that lie ahead. Conclude with a traditional prayer, such as the one commonly known as the Grace before Meals. Here's an example of what this might look like:

Husband: Lord, thank you for letting the meeting with Paul go so well today. You know how worried I was. Thank you for letting that all work out.
Wife: And, God, thank you for letting us be together for dinner tonight, when we've been so busy lately. Please help our son with his practice tonight. Let him do well.

Husband: For these and all our intentions we pray.

Husband and Wife and Family: Bless us, O Lord, and these thy gifts, which we are about to receive from thy bounty, through Christ our Lord. Amen.

This simple and brief period of prayer allows mealtime to be a time of grace where we connect around the things that really matter. It reminds us that God deserves a seat at our marriage and family table.

Evening Prayer

As the day comes to a close, consider reconnecting with each other in prayer, to process all the things that happened throughout the day. This depends, of course, on your schedule and when you have decided to have prayer as a couple. You could use the approach we described in our discussion on morning prayer. There is no evening offering that is similar to the Morning Offering, but you can use your Liturgy of the Hours book or app to pray Night Prayer together.

If you want a less formal option, you might start your evening couple prayer time with a brief opening prayer (technically called a "collect") such as this:

Lord, thank you for the blessings of this day, for carrying us through the challenges we faced and bringing us back to each other now. Help us hear your voice more clearly as you speak to us through the events of today, and help us support each other as we try harder to coop-erate with your grace tomorrow. Let us use everything we have and everything we are to glorify you.

After your opening prayer, take a few moments to reflect together on the following questions:

- When did you feel closest to God? When was it hardest to feel connected to him?
- What do you wish you had handled better, and how do you think you would respond differently, by God's grace, if you were to deal with similar situations tomorrow?
- What was God trying to say to you through the blessings and challenges of the day?
- How is God asking you to grow?
- What support might you need from each other to feel more confident about handling the challenges tomorrow brings or being more aware of all the ways God is blessing you?

Finally, summarize your conversation in prayer as you bring your reflections to God. For instance:

Lord, thank you for helping Lisa feel better today, and please continue healing her of her cold.

Thank you for letting Greg finish that project he's been working on and letting it turn out so well.

Thank you for all the little ways you showed us how much you love us, especially with the beautiful weather today and the wonderful meal we were able to have together as a family. That was so nice to have everyone together.

Help us respond to your call in our hearts. Through all the things going on in our lives, we hear you telling us to trust you more, to rest in you, to not be anxious. But it can be so hard to remember this in the middle of everything. Please give us the grace to support each other in trusting you more.

In addition, we ask your blessing on all those who need our prayers, especially our friend _____ , and for the Church, our nation, and the intentions of the Holy Father.

Give us a good night's rest, Lord. And help us wake up refreshed and ready to serve you in all that we do. Amen.

We like this format because it speaks to the purpose of prayer as a couple—union with God and each other. Prayer like this can lead to deeper intimacy in your marriage, drawing God, you, and your spouse into more graceful communion. Devotions like the Rosary, Divine Mercy Chaplet, scriptural meditations, and other prayers that are personally meaningful to you can also be used for evening prayer—either before, after, or, instead, of the above. Whatever you do, the point is to carve out a little time at the end of each day to reflect on how God is moving in your lives and your marriage and to bring your marriage to him, so that you can be a blessing to each other and the world.

Reflection Questions

- Do you currently conclude your day with prayer? If so, how might you include your spouse in what you already do?
- Are the suggestions for evening prayer similar to or different from your usual approach to prayer? If different, what do you think this kind of prayer would add to your spiritual life as a couple? If similar, how might you use these ideas to make your prayer time even more meaningful?

We hope this chapter has given you a potential framework for daily prayer as a couple, as well as some new ideas for prayer and validation of the ways you already pray. As you begin to explore various prayer options, we'd like to recommend one of our favorite resources for prayer as a couple and family, *Catholic Household Blessings and Prayers*, published by the United States Conference of Catholic Bishops. It is chock-full of wonderful prayers that will help you bring your work and school life, holiday traditions, special needs and concerns, and other aspects of marriage and family life to God in prayer. We use it during the Advent and Christmas seasons, for example, to bless our Advent wreath, Christmas tree, and nativity scene. No home should be without this wonderful resource.

CHAPTER SIX

Praying about Decisions
(Big and Small)

How do you and your spouse make decisions? What
role does God play in your decision-making conversations? Scripture tells us that God loves us and cares about
us so much that the very hairs on our head are numbered
(see Luke 12:7). Because God cares about every part of
your life, there is no decision too small to submit to him.

We aren't suggesting, however, that you enter into a
serious process of discernment about what to eat for dinner or what hairstyle to get. If you pray a morning offering, you have already brought the simple tasks of everyday
life to God. You can trust that he has blessed you with the
intelligence, wisdom, and ability to make good decisions
about daily things.

Even so, our lives are filled with decisions that can ben-
efit from graceful counsel. Some of these decisions have
seemingly small consequences, like whether we should
allow the kids to play baseball this year or, instead, have
more time for family or schoolwork. And some of these
decisions could have serious consequences, like whether we
should take that job or what kind of medical care would
be the best response to a serious illness.

Reflection Questions

- What decisions are you currently facing as a couple or family?
- What are you doing as a couple to ask God to guide you as you make those decisions?

Discernment

As we discussed in chapter 3, when we practice discernment, we invite God into our decision-making process. We engage in the art of listening in prayer. As we do so, we typically find that discernment plays out in one of three—or a combination of three—approaches.

First, sometimes God speaks to us by knocking us off our feet, so to speak. This is rare, but it happens.

Second, sometimes God speaks to us and leads us in our decision making as we gather information, pray about what we have discovered, and reflect upon that prayer.

Third, sometimes God leads us in our decision making through use of our reason. He gave us good heads, and he likes us to use them! In this case, it is enough to bring our reason to God and trust that his grace is fueling our power to make good decisions, even in the absence of profound spiritual feeling.

God is always present. If we are doing our best to bring our decisions to him, get good information, and seek appropriate counsel when necessary, we can step out confidently using the faculties he has given us.

Discernment as a Couple

We should never pursue discernment involving weighty decisions on our own. It's always best to have a mentor, or at least a good spiritual peer, who will pray with us and help us sort through the various feelings we have and facts we have gathered.

A spiritual director can be a wonderful resource when we are discerning God's will for a particular path, such as the choice of a vocation or whether or not to relocate for a job. A spiritual director is a mature Christian person, ordained or lay, who has special training for this role and is steeped in the spiritual wisdom of the Church and the works of Christian spiritual masters. A good spiritual director can be a priceless asset when we are trying to make a serious decision.

But whether or not you are blessed to have a good spiritual director, your spouse is your best partner in prayerful discernment. In the first place, you and your spouse are united—or trying to be united—in helping one another become everything you were meant to be. Second, serious decisions impact both of you, so both husband and wife ought to be part of any process—especially any spiritual process—of decision making.

But why, you may ask, do you need to discern things together? Can't you both pray on your own? Well, of course. And you should. But there's a potential problem. When a husband and wife are trying to make a big decision, they often see *different* pieces of the puzzle. Discerning your path together, through prayer and discussion, allows you to figure out how to put those different puzzle pieces together.

For example, husbands and wives sometimes argue about whether it is time to have another baby. Often one spouse will have some very good reasons to have another child, and the other spouse will have some very good reasons not to have another child. The more they pray about these reasons on their own, the more convinced each spouse becomes of the validity of their own personal insights. What's going on? Is God playing a joke? Is one spouse lying or stupid?

Assuming both spouses are sincerely seeking God's will, the answer might be that the mutual struggle for discernment, and as well as the conversation and prayer involved, can deepen the couple's relationship as they bring the pieces of the puzzle together into a godly whole. In order to do this, the couple needs to resist the temptation to polarize the decision. It is rarely a question of "Do we or don't we have another child?" or "Do we or don't we take the job?" or "Do we or don't we let your sickly mother move in with us?" It is more often a question of "What concerns must we address on the way to determining the right time to have the next child?" "What concerns must we address in order to determine whether this job would be a good fit or a bad fit for our family?" "What concerns must we address as we figure out the best way (and place) to care for your mom's physical health?"

The process of discernment avoids polarized "should we or shouldn't we" fights. Instead, we prayerfully discuss how to bring our various concerns, needs, and resources together in a way that will allow us to be the couple God wants us to be and bear witness to the glory of God through our life together.

How Do We Do This?

Sounds great in theory, but how does this actually work in practice? For a thorough look at the process of discernment, we highly recommend the work of Fr. Timothy Gallagher, an expert on Ignatian spirituality and the author of many easy-to-understand books on St. Ignatius's process of spiritual discernment. Barring a more in-depth understanding of this process, the following can serve as a kind of quick-start manual describing some of the basics of discernment as a couple:

Strive for holiness.

This is the most obvious and most often overlooked step. The best day to start learning to speak Russian is not the second day after you find yourself stumbling around Moscow. If you want to speak any language, it's going to take some practice before you get to be good at it. The same is true for discernment.

If you want to be able to hear God's voice clearly about the bigger decisions in your marriage and family life, it's best to have lots and lots of practice listening to God every day. Husbands and wives who regularly attend Mass and the sacraments together, who go to Confession regularly to repent of the sin that blocks the movement of God's grace, who pray together every day, and who seek God's will and ask God to lead them in the small decisions of their everyday life—these couples are in a much better position to confidently hear God's voice than a couple who only starts praying together in the middle of a crisis.

Don't get us wrong. We aren't saying that God favors the first couple over the second. God is equally present and loving to everyone. But the first couple, through practice and attempting to learn the steps of living a holy life—a life set apart for God—is in a better position to confidently hear God than the second couple. Our commitment to practicing daily prayer as a couple enables us to better take in God's grace, hear his voice, and confidently know his will, especially when the proverbial chips are down.

If you haven't been praying together every day, or have been a little lackluster in your effort, that doesn't mean that God won't answer you or that you won't be able to hear him when he does. It just means that you'll need to be a little more patient while you try to tune in and figure it out. When it comes to the spiritual life, it's easy to feel intimidated, like "We'll *never* be *that* couple"—the couple who can be confident in their ability to hear God speak and know his will. Resist that temptation. Begin where you are, keep at it, and trust God. That's all God asks of you. A little effort. A little consistency. And a willingness to trust him to do the rest.

However confident or confused you feel about your prayer life as husband and wife, the first step is to commit to having regular prayer together. Once you do, you'll learn to recognize—little by little—how God speaks to you in your daily life and circumstances, and you will grow more confident of hearing his voice for the big decisions.

Reflection Questions

- When facing big decisions, how could you carve out even a few minutes a day to seek God's will together?
- Can you establish a plan of action now, so that when challenging times come, you can immediately act on that plan?

Be humble.

When we have a problem, we often think we know exactly the right thing to do—if only our spouse (and God) would get out of the way and let us do it!

But if we truly knew the *perfect* answer to problem X, our spouse would most likely agree, and we wouldn't need God. It isn't a sign that we married an idiot (honest) when our spouse, after praying with us and seeking answers, still doesn't agree with what we want to do. It could be a sign that we're not as smart as we think we are and that we don't really have the answer figured out.

In this case, being humble just means that you are allowed to feel favorable toward your preferred solution but obliged to remain open to other options that either your spouse's needs or God's will might dictate. Of course, the fear is that if we don't get the answer we want *the way we want it,* then our need is going to go unmet. But God's plan takes into account both our needs and the needs of our spouse. God may not fulfill the ache in your heart the way you imagined, but if you let him, he will show you a way to meet those needs that will be even more fulfilling—a way that will satisfy the needs of both you and your spouse and draw you into deeper communion with each other and God.

We can't tell you how God will pull off this little miracle for you. But we can tell you, both from our own experience and from working with hundreds of other couples, that if you approach this process with the commitment we spoke of and the humility we're addressing now, he will lead you to the answer. So how do you do it?

Instead of trying to spend all your energy convincing your spouse how right you are—as you either speak or pray together—discernment works best if you pray together in humility, saying something like this:

> *Lord, this is the desire of my heart. If it is not from you, then please remove it. If it is from you, then please let it grow. Just as important, please help my spouse and me find ways to satisfy this ache in my heart that are respectful of the desires you have placed in my spouse's heart and that fulfill the plan you have for our lives.*

Assuming your spouse has a different perspective, he or she might offer up a similar prayer. For instance,

Wife: Lord, I would like to quit my job and come home to be with the kids, but I'm not sure if we could pull it off. I don't want to make myself and everyone crazy about this if you don't want me to do it. If this desire isn't from you, then please take it away and show me what else I can do to satisfy this longing in my heart. But if this desire is from you, let it grow, and please give us a way to fulfill this dream so that our decision respects my husband's concerns for our financial security.

Husband: Lord, I really like the peace and security that having two incomes gives us. My company has been laying off a lot of people lately, and I'm nervous about the future. It helps my peace of mind to know that my wife is working too, but I know this brings difficulties with it. Please show us some way to meet my need for financial security while being faithful to my wife's desire to be more present to the kids. We don't know how to make it work, but we trust that you can show us. Help us be faithful to your call in our lives and create a family life that meets the needs of everyone in this house and is a blessing to you.

If you'd like to add a more formal dimension to this prayer or spend more time reflecting on God's will, you might conclude by saying, "We offer this Rosary for these intentions and for all those who are struggling to know you and your will in their lives."

Approaching discernment with humility doesn't mean sacrificing the desires of your heart, "giving in" to your spouse, and committing yourself to a life of (supposedly) holy misery. Rather, it means bringing your desires to God and letting him teach you how to meet those needs in ways that draw you, your spouse, and God into closer communion with one another. It is only by approaching God in this receptive way that we can learn the lessons God wants to teach us as he guides us down the path to becoming everything that we were created to be.

Reflection Questions

- When do you tend to be more committed to getting your own way in prayer and in discussions with your spouse than to discovering God's will *together* with your spouse?
- What would you and your spouse need to do in order to consider the longings of one another's heart more humbly?

Gather new information and brainstorm.

In between praying about these serious matters, spend time gathering information and brainstorming new possibilities, no matter how ridiculous they may seem at first. Let's return to the previous couple, who is discerning whether they can afford to have the wife be at home full-time.

After praying, the couple could look closely at their budget to see what they might cut back on and how much money they really need to meet their expenses. Perhaps the wife could cut the food bill by being more diligent about finding coupons and shopping sales. Maybe the husband could search out realistic home-based business opportunities.

Some of these ideas might seem completely absurd, and some might seem terrific; but as this couple continues to talk about everything they have discovered and as they bring it all back to prayer, they will see what stands out in their minds and hearts, revealing the next step to take on the road to discovering God's will.

When we are trying to discern a new path forward, we need to give ourselves as many avenues as possible through which we can hear God. By using the time in between prayer to gather new information, to talk about what we've learned, and to continue our individual prayer and reflection, we give God more ways to communicate his will. We open our minds to opportunities that might not have been obvious at the outset.

Sometimes gathering new information means exploring paths that may seem foolish at first but carry little risk to your present course of life and are at least worth investigating. Other times it will mean seeking professional advice from a financial planner, a counselor, a spiritual director, or another helping professional. Other times it will simply involve consciously and prayerfully reflecting—together—on what God has already given you and discussing new ways to put everything together. Regardless, it is your mutual commitment to this ongoing process of discernment that allows you to hear God's voice, know his will, and cooperate with his grace.

On a personal note, this process has everything to do with why you are reading this book today. Years ago Greg felt two separate—and seemingly conflicted—longings in his heart. First, he wanted to be able to work at home as his father did, so that, like his dad, he would be able to be more present to the family. Second, he felt a deep call to serve the Church in a more direct way than through the private counseling practice he had. At the time, it seemed like fulfilling either desire, much less both of them, was an impossible dream. In fact, when we considered these longings in light of the very real need to provide for the family, they seemed utterly ridiculous.

We kept giving these feelings to God, using the process we described previously. When the feelings didn't go away, we decided to take the long view, to keep doing the work we were doing but gather information, investigate, and pray. Step-by-step, God led us through a process that enabled Greg to come home to work—fulfilling his deepest wish to be more present to our children and simultaneously enabling both of us to dedicate ourselves full-time to ministry work. Almost twenty years, twenty books, four nationally syndicated radio programs, two television series, and an internationally recognized pastoral counseling practice later—all run out of our home—we continue to be amazed at the miraculous way God is still unfolding those longings he planted in Greg's heart years ago.

Let's be clear. God did all of this. We could never have imagined it. We had no idea how to start. We didn't have an inside track. We didn't have connections. We had no plan.

Greg had a longing in his heart, and we had both a commitment to a shared prayer life and a desire to do God's will.

There is nothing special about us. We have seen God work similar wonders in the lives of many, many other couples who have dedicated themselves to seeking his will and following his call. God wants to do the same in your life. Bring your desires to him. Through prayer, discussion, testing his will, and gathering all the information you can—opening yourselves to new avenues of grace—God will help you discern your path forward. He will help you create a marriage and family life that will satisfy the longings of your hearts and allow you to be a witness to the world of his love and grace.

Reflection Questions

- What new information do you need to look for as you discern God's will for the questions facing you right now?
- What would you and your spouse need to do to have more effective conversations about the longings of your hearts as you discern how to respond to those longings?

Be patient and persistent.

Discernment as a couple is a *process* that requires patience and persistent prayer and communication. We've touched on this, but it bears repeating, even if only briefly. You need to be committed to working it out over the long haul. You can't just say one day, "God, tell me what to do," and then go on living your life the same way you always have.

Discernment is not just about figuring out what God wants you to do. It is ultimately about uniting your hearts to each other and to him. This is a lifelong process. Be patient with it. Be patient with God. Be patient with yourself. Be patient with each other, and persist in the power of prayer.

Listen to the longings of your heart. Test them through prayer. Be humble enough to let go of the longings that aren't from God. At the same time, open yourself up to having God fulfill the longings that persist in prayer, no matter how crazy they might seem at the time.

Discerning God's will as a couple stands at the heart of your marital vocation. It is an essential prayerful practice that serves, not only the practical purpose of helping you find answers when grappling with questions, but also the spiritual purpose of uniting you as a couple.

Reflection Questions

- Are you ever tempted to stop seeking God's will *before* you are sure of what he is saying to you? How will you resist this temptation and instead persevere until the way is clear?
- Has there ever been a time when you, either individually or as a couple, stuck with prayer until you were sure of God's will?
- What was that like? How could you apply that perseverance to the decisions you face today?

Listen to His Word

As you continue to reflect on ways you and your spouse can hear God's voice speaking more clearly in and through your marriage, consider the verses below from Scripture. Post them around your house. Meditate on them. Let God speak to you through them as you go about your day and as you discern his will for your life and choices.

First, pray in this way:

Lord, you have the words of everlasting life. Make your word plain to us. Open our hearts to your will, and help us to want what you desire for us. We give you our hopes and dreams, and we ask you to take them, remove what is not of you, and grant all that remains in ways that lead us closer to each other and to you. Help my spouse and me make decisions that glorify you in all we do. Amen.

My son, if you receive my words
    and treasure up my commandments with you,
making your ear attentive to wisdom
    and inclining your heart to understanding;
yes, if you cry out for insight
    and raise your voice for understanding,
if you seek it like silver
    and search for it as for hidden treasures;
then you will understand the fear of the LORD
    and find the knowledge of God. (Proverbs 2:1-5,
    RSVCE)

But solid food is for the mature, for those who have their powers of discernment trained by constant practice to distinguish good from evil. (Hebrews 5:14, ESV) If any of you lacks wisdom, let him ask God, who gives to all men generously and without reproaching, and it will be given him. (James 1:5, RSVCE)

But test everything; hold fast what is good. (1 Thessalonians 5:21, RSVCE)

I can do nothing on my own. As I hear, I judge, and my judgment is just, because I seek not my own will but the will of him who sent me. (John 5:30, ESV)

Try to discern what is pleasing to the Lord. (Ephesians 5:10, ESV)

We demolish arguments and every pretension that sets itself up against the knowledge of God, and we take captive every thought to make it obedient to Christ. (2 Corinthians 10:5, NIV)

A Prayer for Discernment

Lord, we give you the longings of our hearts. Help us hear you speaking through these longings—to let go of anything that isn't from you and to hold fast to everything that comes from the promptings of your Holy

Spirit. Help us to be humble in the presence of your call to our hearts, to be open to ways you might wish to fulfill that call in our lives, to be generous to each other even when fulfilling that call stretches or challenges us. Give us the grace we need to be persistent in prayer and committed to seeking your will in all things, that we might be the couple you are calling us to be. St. Ignatius of Loyola, pray for us. Amen.

CHAPTER SEVEN

Praying through Conflict

The Lord GOD has given me a well-trained tongue.
(Isaiah 50:4)

As we explored in the last chapter, discernment is the process of turning our hearts to God, learning to listen to his voice, seeking new information, opening new channels through which his grace might flow, and working through all of this in your marriage by maintaining ongoing commitment, prayer, and communication. But as beautiful as the process sounds in theory, it easily breaks down into conflict.

That isn't necessarily a bad thing. As we point out in our book *For Better . . . FOREVER! The Catholic Guide to Lifelong Marriage,* conflict plays a spiritual as well as a relational role in a healthy, godly marriage. Healthy arguments are simply the means by which our selfishness, imperfections, pettiness, immaturity, and spitefulness are slowly ground away—like a spiritual exfoliation treatment that leaves our souls free of the bumps and blemishes that would make us less appealing in the eyes of the Lord.

A word of caution is in order. If your disagreements with your spouse leave you feeling demeaned, diminished, distant, and reluctant to engage in further conversations about serious matters, or if your arguments become physical in any way, please seek professional counseling immediately.

Abuse is never appropriate, least of all abuse of the spouse God gave you and expects you to cherish. It is not God's will for you, your spouse, or your relationship.

Before You Begin

With that note in mind, it's important to realize that marital conflict does not have to separate you from God. In fact, it can be an opportunity to invite God into the process, so that he might teach you how to grow closer together through your arguments rather than in spite of them.

Eli Finkel, a psychologist and researcher at Northwestern University, describes a technique he teaches couples called "The Marriage Hack." Before couples engage in a potentially heated discussion about a difficult topic, he asks them to take a moment to imagine the advice that someone who loves both members of the couple and wishes them both well might give for resolving the disagreement. Then, and only then, should the couple begin their conversation. Research found that this simple exercise not only helped couples resolve conflict more peaceably and effectively but actually improved their overall sense of marital well-being when compared with couples who did not use this technique in their arguments.[11]

Christian couples don't have to imagine such an advisor. He exists! God loves you both, and he will help you learn to resolve your disagreements in a manner that is good for both of you. To that end, consider doing a "marriage hack" before entering into a challenging discussion.

Next, pray. Aristotle once wrote, "Well begun is half done." If you want your disagreements to produce effective resolutions to your problems, there is no better way to begin than by bringing your hearts, desires, and concerns to God. Ideally, you will remember to do this before, during, and after the tension starts. But even if you only remember to invite God to be part of the discussion at one of these points, we promise—as we have found in both our personal and professional experience—that with his help, you can learn to transform your arguments. They will feel less like boxing matches and more like deep-muscle massages—uncomfortable at the time but, ultimately, making your relationship closer, more relaxed, and more limber.

If you pray on your own before initiating a potentially difficult conversation, simply call to mind the fact that God loves you and your spouse and wants what's best for both of you. Then, in your own words, ask God to help you advocate clearly for your needs, even as you work hard to respect your spouse's needs, treating your husband or wife with love and understanding. You might say something like "Lord, I don't want to have this conversation, but I feel that I have to. Please help me to keep my head clear and to focus on finding answers to the things that frustrate me. Help me to approach my spouse with the love and understanding that come from your heart and to work hard to incorporate my partner's needs into any plans we make moving forward." Then begin the conversation, confident that you will be guided by grace.

If your spouse is willing to pray with you before you begin your conversation, sit down together, hold hands if possible, and take turns asking for God's help. Here's an example of what such prayer might look like:

Husband: Lord, this is hard. This is a hard topic to discuss peacefully, and there are many things to keep in mind. Help us be faithful to our own concerns, be sensitive to each other's needs, remember to love each other through it all, and ultimately work together to find the answers you want for us.

Wife: Lord, you know how much I hate talking about this. But we place our trust in you. Help us remember that we love each other, that we want what's best for each other, and that the most important thing is to take care of each other while we try to figure out what you want us to do. We place our trust in you, Lord. Lead us and guide us to a peaceful solution. Holy Family, pray for us. Amen.

Whatever words you use, keep it short, heartfelt, humble, and loving. Don't try to lecture your spouse with your prayer or spiritually "stack the deck" by using your portion of the prayer to tell God all about how wonderful your ideas for solving the problem would be if only your idiot spouse would just listen to you already.

Instead remember to ask *specifically* for God's help in finding a solution that reflects the most important concerns of each of you and is rooted in God's will for your marriage. Ask for an extra measure of grace, especially if one or both of you start to feel stuck. Finally, ask God to help you encourage each other through the tension and toward effective, godly solutions. And for good measure, asking the Holy Family to pray for you never hurt anyone.

Prayer isn't magic. The conversation will still be hard. You will still have to focus on being respectful, taking care of each other through the conflict, advocating for yourself, and working hard to understand and respect your spouse's needs. If you need better arguing skills, you should seek professional help to get them. In fact, expecting God to magically make up for some personal deficiency that we are too lazy to address is known as the *sin of presumption*. You *will* need to spend time and energy overcoming your deficits. God may certainly work miracles whenever he wishes, but obstinately *requiring* him to give us a miraculous infusion of conflict resolutions skills, instead of doing our best to go out and get those skills, does not reflect the heart of an intentional disciple.

Although prayers such as these won't give you all the skills you need to solve your problems, Christians can have confidence that, in the words of St. Thomas Aquinas, "Grace builds on nature."[12] We can be assured that praying before any event will give us the grace we need to make the best use of whatever skills we have. And if that sounds like faint praise, remember that God used five loaves and two fish to feed over five thousand people. He can do a lot with the very little we give him, and it is good to be confident in his power. Just don't be so confident that you presumptuously refuse to do everything you could to cooperate with all that grace God is pouring out.

Reflection Questions

- Have you ever prayed, either alone or together, before initiating a difficult conversation with someone?
- What was that experience like for you? What difference did it make?

When Conflict Heats Up

Despite our best efforts and prayers, sometimes our disagreements will start to go off the rails. Tempers may flare, discussions can become polarized, and frustrations can build. It can be tremendously helpful in these times to step back and seek a spiritual course correction.

The idea of praying in the middle of a conflict can seem odd to people. When you're angry with your spouse, perhaps the only way you could imagine praying in the middle of an argument is to take out a cross and some holy water and proclaim, "Out! Demon spirits of stupidity, I command you. Come out of my spouse!"

Obviously, that's not quite the prayer we have in mind (and we don't recommend trying it). Perhaps the best way to describe what we're talking about is to share a story of a time when praying in the middle of an argument was particularly helpful to us.

It shouldn't come as a surprise (but somehow, to many people it still does) that we disagree fairly often as a couple. We're different people, after all. Fortunately, we're able to handle most of those disagreements pretty well. Still, we're not beyond yelling at each other from time to time. We're not proud of that, but we'd be lying if we said it never happened.

One day we were having what was, for us, a pretty nasty argument. Neither of us remembers what it was about, but clearly it mattered deeply at the time. We weren't hearing each other. We both felt more than a little attacked and misunderstood. And there was a fair amount of yelling involved.

Greg: I remember thinking, "We just keep going in circles. I have no idea how to get her to see what I'm saying, and all I want to do is scream louder and louder until she figures it out." I knew that wasn't going to work. Finally, I just threw up my hands and shouted, "I'm done. I can't do this. I need a break." And I stormed out of the house. I can probably count on one hand the number of times I've done that, and I know it really infuriated Lisa, but I just couldn't take it anymore. I was afraid of what would come out of my mouth if I stayed there.

We have a pond on our property, and there's a big rock next to it. I went over there, sat down, and started praying. It was hardly the most elegant prayer, but it was real. I said something like, "Lord, I've never been so furious in my entire life. I swear to you, all I want to do is get in my car, drive, and never come back. Somehow I know that's not what you want me to do, but for the life of me, I don't know what you want or how you expect me to fix this. You better help me figure something out, because so help me, I've had it. I'm stuck. I don't know how to love her in this. I don't know how to give her what she wants from me. I don't even really know what that is. I sure as heck don't know how to get her to see what I need out of all this. Please help. I don't know what to do."

And then I just sat there, staring at the pond, half praying, half just trying to stop seeing red and hoping—I don't know what—that I'd get some kind of sign, I guess.

Lisa: Well, when he stormed out, honestly, I was fit to be tied. I couldn't believe he'd take off on me like that. I wasn't about to chase after him though. "Fine," I thought. "He wants to stomp off? Let him. I'm not about to go chasing after him, the big jerk."

I marched into the bedroom, trying to decide whether I should fold the laundry or just throw it out the window. That's when I happened to look out the window that overlooks our pond. I saw Greg sitting there, and I could tell he was praying.

I'll be honest. The first thought that popped into my head was "Oh, that's just perfect. He's praying! He's probably telling God about what a witch I am. Who does he think he is anyway? He's the one who walks out of here, and he thinks he can get brownie points with God by praying? Well, he's got another thing coming." And then I started praying, because I wanted to make sure God heard my side of the story too.

Greg: About ten or fifteen minutes after I left the house, I had this strong sense it was time to go back. I really didn't want to. I just wanted to keep hiding. But I felt that God was pulling my hand and saying, "Come on. Time to get back in there."

I stood up and started walking toward the house, when all of a sudden, I saw the front door open and Lisa coming out. I cringed internally. I really still had no idea what to say, and I was terrified that we were just going to pick up where we left off. But I also remember feeling that somehow, with God's grace, we'd be able to work it out.

Lisa: When I got done ranting at God, I felt spent. I was still upset, but I felt embarrassed and foolish too. I knew we were better than this. I wasn't sure what to do, but I knew we weren't going to get anywhere just pouting in our own corners, waiting for the other one to blink. I was really glad when I opened the door to go outside and saw that Greg was already starting to walk back to the house.

Greg: The timing of that was a little miracle, honestly. We met halfway, and I remember saying, "Look, I'm really sorry about all this. I don't know how to get through this, but I love you, and I don't want to fight."

Lisa: I told him that I loved him and didn't want to fight either. We tentatively held hands and walked back in the house. And sure enough, we really were able to sort things out—not just move past it but really come to a better place about the stuff we were upset about. Honestly though, it wasn't us. It was all God.

Greg: That certainly wasn't the first time either of us had prayed in the middle of a fight, and it wasn't the last. It was just one of the more memorable times. But it illustrated for us how God doesn't just want the pretty parts of our relationship. He really does want to be there with us in the middle of the mess. We just have to invite him to help us clean it up. There has never been a time when we have invited God into our arguments when he hasn't come through in a major way.

Other times, when we manage to do a better job at catching ourselves early, we're able to prevent things from becoming this dramatic. When things start heating up, one of us will stop and say, "Look, clearly this isn't working. Let's just take a minute to pray, OK?" And then we pray some version of, "Lord, we don't know how to get through to each other. We're both convinced that we're right. We both know what we want. Help us work together to figure out what you want. Help us get through this as peacefully as possible and sort everything out according to your will. Amen."

Most times that's enough. It doesn't always go perfectly after that, but it goes better. At the very least, God gives us the grace to remember that there are bigger things at stake than our momentary feelings and desires. He helps us see the big picture, and while that doesn't diminish our present needs, it does help us have a sense of perspective about them and a flexibility we wouldn't have if we were left to our own devices.

Reflection Questions

- What difference would it make if you habitually invited God into your arguments?
- If you don't currently pray together before or during difficult conversations, how can you suggest this to your spouse, so that the next time a disagreement arises, you have agreed ahead of time to stop and pray?

After the Fight

Life isn't a sitcom. Sometimes disputes don't get wrapped up in under thirty minutes, complete with an adorable ending and a moral. OK, maybe more than sometimes. That's where prayer after conflict comes in. Perhaps you've said all you know how to say, and you've run out of steam, but you still aren't any closer to a solution. In our experience, this is the point at which most couples say, "Well, I guess *that* will never change. I suppose I should just let it go."

The truth is, there *are* some things you should let go of. If you're arguing about some petty preference or even a relatively small act of thoughtlessness that probably won't happen again, then "offering it up" to God can be a useful practice that helps you grow in patience, understanding, and self-control—all good things.

Then again, for many issues, perhaps even for most issues, this is either impossible or inadvisable. Just trying to keep your mouth shut and not complain about a problem because the last conversation didn't go so well is a recipe for disaster. Couples who adopt this approach usually end up talking less and less about more and more, until they have virtually nothing to say to each other about almost anything. One of our favorite quotes is by Pope St. Gregory the Great: "Thoughts seethe all the more when corralled by the violent guard of an indiscreet silence." Truer words were never uttered. The more we try to not talk about certain frustrations, the worse those frustrations tend to get.

Praying after the argument can help you get both the space and the perspective you need, as well as the determination to stick with it until the issue is truly resolved—even if that takes days, weeks, months, or even years of periodic reengagement of the issue. This post-argument prayer could involve a Rosary or chaplet for the intention of finding a godly resolution to your disagreement. Or you might ask for the intercession of the Holy Family or other married saints, like Louis and Zélie Martin, the parents of St. Thérèse of Lisieux. Or you might use your own words, such as:

Lord, thank you for getting us this far. We don't really know how to resolve this, but we trust you that you will help us sort it out in time. Help us to listen to each other, to reflect on what the other says, and to be genuinely thoughtful about the ways we might work together to meet each other's needs.

Help us to be generous and willing to change as we find godly solutions that ask us to grow. We place our trust in you, Lord Jesus. Make us the husband and wife to each other that you want us to be.

Reflection Questions

- What difference would praying together at the conclusion of a problem-solving discussion make?
- What steps do you need to take to incorporate this habit into your marriage?

Here Comes the Sun!

What about the Scripture that says, "Do not let the sun set on your anger" (Ephesians 4:26)? It is our position that St. Paul didn't intend to suggest that a couple's issues needed to be resolved before they went to bed or, worse, that a couple should stay up until the wee hours of "oh-dark-thirty" getting more exhausted and angry in a flawed attempt to wrap up their disagreements before their heads hit the pillow.

In fact, the first half of the passage from Ephesians says, "Be angry but do not sin." As we point out in our book *Broken Gods: Hope, Healing, and the Seven Longings of the Human Heart*, anger can be righteous if it leads to a proportionate, appropriate, and productive response to a problem. On the other hand, anger can become sinful (that is, wrath) if it pushes us toward disproportionate, inappropriate, and unproductive responses to the same. When St. Paul says, "Be angry but do not sin; do not let the sun set on your anger," he isn't saying, "Make sure you get your messes cleaned up before dawn." He is simply reminding the faithful, "Don't give in to sinful anger, and if you are tempted to wrath, get it under control ASAP."

That's good advice. By all means, if you have an impulse to yell, lecture, shame, scream, or sell your spouse on eBay (we're kidding about the last one), then you should definitely get that under control before you go to bed. But at the same time, it's perfectly OK to recognize that some issues will be easier to resolve after a good night's sleep.

It isn't unusual to have to wrestle with particular disagreements for years. We certainly have. And as long as those disagreements can be respectful and don't start spoiling the rest of your relationship, then that's just marriage. Take your time. Pray. Engage. Argue. Take a break. Pray again. Repeat. Eventually, you'll get to where you need to go.

Nevertheless, if a particular disagreement, or number of disagreements, or the *way* you disagree is starting to keep you up at night, causing you to discuss less and less or making it harder for you to enjoy each other's company, then it is time to seek professional help. Do not commit the sin of presumption by begging God for a change but never doing anything to facilitate the changes that are necessary. It isn't enough to pray; we must also do. Grace builds on nature. It doesn't stand in place of it. Get the help you need to receive the fullness of all the blessings God wants to give you.

There are many excellent marriage-building resources available, from self-help books to programs like Retrouvaille (www.HelpOurMarriage.com). Greg's book *How to Heal Your Marriage and Nurture Lasting Love* examines the habits healthy couples practice to effectively resolve conflict. And again, we and our associate counselors are available to help you through the Pastoral Solutions Institute's Catholic telecounseling practice. Please don't hesitate to reach out to us at www.CatholicCounselors.com or by calling 740-266-6461.

Reflection Questions

- Does the discussion of the passage "Do not let the sun set on your anger" change the way you approach marital disputes?
- If you have become aware of the need to get new problem-solving skills, how will you get them?

What If My Spouse Won't Do These Things?

As we said earlier, if your spouse is completely hostile or closed to these ideas and not at least willing to join you as he or she is able—even if that only means maintaining a respectful silence while you pray in front of them—then you do not have a religion problem in your marriage. You have a respect problem, which will most likely require counseling to resolve.

Short of this level of animosity, however, have courage. Prayer is as essential to effective conflict resolution as breathing and talking and changing. Don't be afraid to simply say to your spouse, "I really need to pray about this with you. I don't want to pressure you. Just please join with me however you can." Then start. Don't ask permission. Don't feel bad. You are doing a good thing, the best thing. Just do it.

If that is your situation—you are praying alone in front of your spouse—then later, when you aren't arguing about that issue, circle back around to the discussion, and ask your spouse how he or she feels when you pray during these times. What are they thinking about while you're praying? Do they have any questions about why it is so important to you to turn to God in these times?

Take advantage of these naturally occurring opportunities to witness to your spouse—not lecture—about the role that your faith plays in your everyday life. Don't be afraid to tell your spouse how much it would mean to you to have them take a more active role. Ask them what they might need from you to make that happen. Ask this question gently and respectfully but with the attitude that you are asking them the most reasonable thing in the world. *Because you are.* You don't need to apologize for your faith, hide it under a bushel basket, or feel guilty about it. Be not afraid!

Tying It All Together

This chapter builds upon the discernment chapter by proposing approaches to help you move forward when discernment gets tough and your prayer life and problem-solving conversations get off track. But this chapter also assumes that as long as you have an open issue that needs to be addressed, you continue to discuss it and discern God's will about it when you are not arguing.

Many couples fail to discuss issues—or pray about them—unless they are fed up and arguing. These couples have marriages that, over time, comes to resemble guerilla warfare. Everything is fine. The village is peaceful. Suddenly shots ring out. Buildings burn. Carnage ensues. And then the combatants fade back into the jungle, while the villagers go back to pretending that life is perfectly normal.

This is not a Christian approach to discernment and conflict resolution. This is cowardly. It is slothful. It is presumptuous. In our practice and on our radio program, we encounter too many spouses who have been miserable for years in their marriage. They say, "I pray, and I pray, and nothing ever changes. I try to offer my sufferings up to God, but nothing ever changes. I guess my marriage is my cross."

Your marriage is not your cross, at least not in this sense. Your marriage is absolutely your and your spouse's best means of sanctification *if you do the work that your marriage requires*. This begins with individual prayer and prayer together. God's grace will flow from this prayer life and bear fruit in your ongoing commitment to discernment, communication, and growth in love and generosity. That is how prayer works.

As we bring this chapter to a close, here are several verses of Scripture that you and your spouse can pray about and reflect upon as you look for more graceful approaches to resolving disagreement and conflict.

Begin with a prayer. Here are some suggestions:

Lord, we bring our hearts to you. Speak to us through your word. Help us cultivate listening ears, compassionate hearts, and generous spirits, that we may be able to grow and change together and help each other become the people—the saints—you are calling us to be. Holy Family, pray for us.

Lord Jesus Christ, let your word be in our hearts and on our lips. Help us approach the disagreements we face in our marriage with courageous faith, compassion, mutual respect, self-control, and a genuine desire to love each other even more than we want to get our own way. Let our disagreements be the preparation chamber for the eternal wedding feast that will remove our spiritual, emotional, and psychological imperfections and allows us to stand under your gaze in joyful confidence, knowing that we are beautiful in every way in your sight. We ask this through Christ our Lord and through the intercession of the Holy Family. Amen.

A hot-tempered person stirs up conflict, but the one who is patient calms a quarrel. (Proverbs 15:18, NIV)

Better a patient person than a warrior, one with self-control than one who takes a city. (Proverbs 16:32, NIV)

Do not be quickly provoked in your spirit, for anger resides in the lap of fools. (Ecclesiastes 7:9, NIV)

Avoid foolish and ignorant debates, for you know that they breed quarrels. A slave of the Lord should not quarrel, but should be gentle with everyone. (2 Timothy 2:23-24)

"But I tell you that anyone who is angry with a brother or sister will be subject to judgment. Again, anyone who says to a brother or sister, 'Raca,' is answerable to the court. And anyone who says, 'You fool!' will be in danger of the fire of hell." (Matthew 5:22, NIV)

But now you must also rid yourselves of all such things as these: anger, rage, malice, slander, and filthy language from your lips. (Colossians 3:8, NIV)

"If your brother or sister sins, go and point out their fault, just between the two of you. If they listen to you, you have won them over. But if they will not listen, take one or two others along, so that 'every matter may be established by the testimony of two or three witnesses.'" (Matthew 18:15-16, NIV)

CHAPTER EIGHT

Praying through Challenging Times

Consider it all joy, my brothers, when you encounter various trials, for you know that the testing of your faith produces perseverance. And let perseverance be perfect, so that you may be perfect and complete, lacking in nothing. (James 1:2-4)

When husbands and wives vow to remain faithful for better or for worse, in sickness and in health, for richer or for poorer, we hope that we will have more of the former than the latter. But every marriage involves plenty of both.

There is a saying, "When hard times come through the door, love flies out the window." Sadly, there is some truth to this, insofar as it is not unusual for couples and families to turn on each other when they encounter challenges. When we are under attack, we tend to want to comfort ourselves. When we are stressed, we become angry or worse with people who dare to have feelings or needs that are different from ours—or who require us to take care of them. It can be very difficult to stick close to each other, much less grow closer, through trial.

And yet that is exactly what we are called to do as husbands and wives. Remember God's words at the beginning of time: "It is not good for the man to be alone" (Genesis 2:18)! Satan, who is like an angry lion waiting to devour us (see 1 Peter 5:8), wants to divide husbands and wives because we are easier prey when we are alone.

Like most couples, we have seen many times in our marriage when troubles piled up and fear, anger, and self-protection threatened to take hold. Despite all the psychological tools and resources at our disposal, we can honestly say that, in many of those times, our commitment to prayer together did the most to keep us from turning against each other. Of course, all the things we wrote in the discernment and praying through conflict chapters applied to these times as well. But praying as a couple through challenging times is crucial. Here are a few ways you can pray:

Dayenu

The Jewish people sing a song during the Passover celebration that tells the story of all the ways God has been present to them. The song is *Dayenu* (die-AY-noo), which means "It would have been enough." The lyrics vary, but the song is based on incidents the Israelites encountered on their exodus from Egypt. For example,

> *If you had divided the sea for us but had not taken us through it on dry land, it would have been enough for us. If you had led us through the sea but had not given us a pillar of fire in the desert, it would have been enough for us.*

If you had led us with a pillar of fire but had not given us
water from the rock, it would have been enough for us.
If you had given us water from the rock but had not
fed us with manna in the desert, it would have been
enough for us.

And so on.

In difficult times in our lives together, we create our own personal *dayenu* prayer. This is similar to the "sacrifice of praise" we discussed in an earlier chapter but broader. Instead of merely searching for immediate blessings for which to be grateful, the *dayenu* prayer forces us to intentionally call to mind all the times, from the earliest days of our relationship, that God delivered us from some terrible thing we faced. We take turns mentioning specific incidents of sickness, serious financial crises, and other dangers and pressures we have endured. We don't worry about listing things in order. Our primary purpose is to remind ourselves of God's faithfulness in the past, when we were sure we were doomed.

Lisa: It would have been enough if you healed me from
my serious illness, but you gave Greg the grace to take
care of everything without losing his mind.
Greg: It would have been enough if you had given me
the grace to keep it together when Lisa was so sick, but
you helped us both be present to the kids.
Lisa: It would have been enough if you had helped us
stay present to the kids when we were going through

*that time when I was sick, but you kept us safe through
our car accident.*

*Greg: It would have been enough if you had kept us
safe through our car accident, but you took care of us
when I lost my job.*

*Lisa: It would have been enough if you had taken care
of us when Greg lost his job, but . . .*

You get the idea. Psychologically, a marital *dayenu* like
this helps you put whatever you're going through in perspective. Spiritually, it reminds you of God's faithfulness
through trial, and it challenges you to remember that even
though you were sure that God had tired of taking care
of you a million times before, he always came through.

Relationally, this prayer reminds you of all the things
you have been through together and the life you have man-
aged to create together—through God's grace—in spite of
it all. It reminds you of the times you bore up well, and it
reminds you of the times you didn't; and it challenges you
to do better, to hang tough and stick together. A marital
dayenu is a powerful way to witness to each other about
God's mercy in your lives and to promise to stand together
through this trial as well.

Reflection Questions

- If you were to develop your own marital *dayenu* prayer,
  what situations would you list?

- Do you think it would make a difference if you and your spouse were to remind each other of God's past faithfulness whenever you hit challenging times in your life or relationship? In what ways?

The Sorrowful Mysteries of the Rosary

The Rosary offers us the opportunity to draw closer to Jesus as we meditate on his life through its mysteries. We can place ourselves, in spirit, as witnesses to these important events in the life of the Lord and imagine what it would have been like to be there.

When we go through difficult times, it can be hard to find the right words to say. On top of this, even if we know intellectually that God is present in our struggles, sometimes it's hard to feel as if God understands what we're going through. Praying the sorrowful mysteries together can be a powerful way of remembering that God is present, not only in the good times, but also in the most challenging hardships we face.

As you pray, place yourself inside the scene depicted by each mystery. Don't compare your sufferings with Jesus' sufferings—that's not what we're suggesting—and definitely don't feel guilty about your own troubles in light of what he endured. Rather, let yourself identify your sufferings with the sufferings of Christ, as a reminder that God can use your pain for good and that there is a resurrection after the cross.

Feel free to be creative about how you place yourself inside the mystery. Perhaps you will simply observe as Jesus endures the suffering described. Perhaps you will imagine yourself experiencing the mystery from the perspective of Christ or one of the other people present. Or you might simply imagine how your own present suffering allows you to understand, on an emotional level, the incredible love that Jesus poured out for you through his suffering. Use your imagination. As St. Ignatius of Loyola noted, our imaginations are powerful tools for prayer.

We've provided some examples to get you started. Discuss the questions (or share any other reflections) at the end of each mystery. Don't focus on "getting the whole prayer done." If you run out of time, that's OK. It is better to have a more meaningful prayer time than one that checks off all the right boxes but lacks depth, intimacy, and connection with God and your spouse.

The First Sorrowful Mystery: The Agony in the Garden

What is it like to wait on God's will or God's deliverance as you go through your present struggles? How does the pain you feel while you wait help you relate in a new way to Christ's agony in the garden? What does Christ's experience in the garden teach you and your spouse about waiting together for God's glory to be revealed in your marriage?

The Second Sorrowful Mystery:
The Scourging at the Pillar

When going through hard times, there are almost always additional unpleasant surprises: new, frustrating developments that, like another lash on the back, rip open the wounds and bring a fresh experience of pain. What are the most challenging aspects of this experience you and your spouse are going through? How can these sufferings help you relate to the scourging Christ willingly endured out of love for you and your spouse?

The Third Sorrowful Mystery:
The Crowning with Thorns

It wasn't enough for the Romans to inflict physical pain on Jesus. They mocked him by dressing him up as a king with a crown of thorns. When we go through hard times, we often feel ashamed. Is the current suffering in your life bringing feelings of shame or embarrassment? How can you bring these feelings to God, so that he can love you through them, instead of turning on each other in your desire to protect yourselves?

The Fourth Sorrowful Mystery:
The Carrying of the Cross

Sometimes when we are enduring the struggle, we stumble and fall. We need the support of someone who isn't afraid to help us ease our burdens, our own Simon of Cyrene. How are you and your spouse trying to ease each other's burdens during the trial you are enduring? Is there something more you could do? What would that be specifically?

The Fifth Sorrowful Mystery: The Crucifixion

When Jesus exclaimed, "My God, my God, why have you forsaken me?" (Matthew 27:46), he was not despairing. He was praying Psalm 22, which begins with those words but ends with a defiant proclamation of victory over evil.

And I will live for the LORD;
my descendants will serve you.
The generation to come will be told of the Lord,
that they may proclaim to a people yet unborn
the deliverance you have brought. (Psalm 22:31-32)

It is easy to feel crushed by the sufferings we experience. How will you and your spouse encourage each other to remain defiantly hopeful in God's grace and providence, even in the face of the pain you are currently experiencing?

Do you see what a powerful prayer this can be? These reflections, as well as others you and your spouse may develop, allow you to come together, not in spite of your sufferings, but through your sufferings. And they remind you that the challenge for any Christian couple is not merely to endure suffering but to use our inevitable sufferings as opportunities to care for one another. When all our protections are stripped away, and our defenses are laid bare, we see that God is still present—on his own and through our spouse.

Reflection Questions

- Do you think that seeing your sufferings in light of the sorrowful mysteries will help you? What difference might it make in your marriage?
- How might praying this way during hard times challenge you and your spouse to stand together more effectively than you have in the past?

The Three-Ply Cord

Where one alone may be overcome, two together can resist. A three-ply cord is not easily broken. (Ecclesiastes 4:12)

A rope of only one or two cords frays easily. Similarly, your marriage will fray if you try to deal with the pain of life on your own, with only the resources you and your spouse can bring to the table. But uniting yourselves to God in your suffering creates "a three-ply cord" that "is not easily broken."

The examples we have given so far in this chapter offer different ways to create this three-ply cord. They allow you to "tie off" and keep climbing the mountain when the going gets tough. Another way to create this three-ply cord is simply to ask God for the grace to create it. You should feel free to use your own words, but here is an example to get you started:

Husband: Lord, we're really struggling, and each of us is worn out from this experience. And there doesn't seem to be an end in sight. We trust in you, and we ask you to deliver us quickly. And while we wait for you, please help us be a three-ply cord. Strengthen us. Make us the couple we need to be through this trial. Help us to love each other well and to remind each other of the gift that our marriage is meant to be, especially in hard times.

Wife: Lord, make me the wife my husband needs me to be. Help me be a real helpmate and partner. Help me be willing to grow and stretch in all the ways I need to, in order to be the woman you need me to be for him. And in those times when I don't feel as if I'm enough, please love him through me.

Husband: And make me the husband my wife needs me to be. Help me be her friend and partner even through the hardest, most frustrating, and scariest parts of all this. Make me willing to grow and stretch in all the ways I need to, in order to be the man you need me to be for her. And in those times when I don't feel like I'm enough, please love her through me. Thank you for this marriage. And thank you for this woman who loves me in good times and bad.

Wife: And thank you for this man who loves me in good times and bad. We give ourselves, our life, and this relationship to you.

Husband: Jesus, we trust in you.

If you like, add your favorite traditional prayers or other expressions of praise, intercession, or supplication. As we have said before, as long as your prayer comes from your heart, there is no wrong way to do it. The point is to resist the temptation to let trials turn you away from God and turn on each other. A prayer such as the one above, said daily for the duration of your struggle, helps you remember that your goal in tough times is to hang on to each other and God with all you have, no matter what.

Of course, there are many ways to pray through difficult times. Neither this book nor this chapter is meant to offer an exhaustive list but rather to inspire you to create ways of connecting with God that are meaningful to you and your spouse.

Reflection Questions

- How do you currently pray with your spouse during tough times?
- Have you ever specifically asked God to make your marriage, in union with him, a three-ply cord? What difference might it make in your relationship?

But What If My Spouse Won't Pray with Me?

All the suggestions we have made for praying through trials with your spouse apply to the spouse who is alone in praying for his or her marriage. The *dayenu* prayer, the marital reflections on the sorrowful mysteries, and even the prayer asking God to make you and your spouse a three-ply cord through trial can be adapted for use by a spouse praying alone for his or her marriage. When we are going through difficult times and have to face those times without the help of a spiritual partner, it is easy to become bitter or resentful toward one's spouse. But praying according to the ways recommended in this chapter can help us reflect on how God is present to us in our suffering and loneliness.

Additionally, we suggest that challenging times create good opportunities to revisit the idea of inviting your spiritually recalcitrant spouse to begin praying with you. In times of crisis, people actively seek resources; they are more receptive than when things are going well and they think they have everything under control.

In any case, know that you are not alone. God walks with you. You are his beloved. Remember the words of the beloved in the Song of Songs, when she was afraid and alone:

> *"Let me rise then and go about the city,*
> *through the streets and squares;*
> *Let me seek him whom my soul loves."*
> *I sought him but I did not find him.*
> *The watchmen found me,*
> *as they made their rounds in the city:*
> *"Him whom my soul loves—have you seen him?"*

Hardly had I left them
 when I found him whom my soul loves.
I held him and would not let him go. (Song of Songs 3:2-4)

God is your beloved. Never doubt his presence. And in those times when you can't help but doubt, rise and seek him. You will find him. And when you do, hold on, and never let him go.

Reflection Questions

- How might you use the challenges you face in your life and relationship as opportunities to invite your spouse to pray with you?
- If you are spiritually alone in your marriage, you have greater resources than your spouse to weather hard times. How might fearlessly tapping into your strength help you be a better support and witness to your spouse?

Listen to His Word

Prayerfully reflect on the following verses. Alone or with your spouse, ask God to speak to you through his word throughout the day. Post these verses in various prominent places, so you can be reminded of God's word when you need it most.

Be strong and courageous. Do not be afraid or terrified because of them, for the LORD *your God goes with* you; he will never leave you nor forsake you. *(Deuteronomy 31:6, NIV)*

Trust in the Lord *with all your heart,*
and do not lean on your own understanding.
In all your ways acknowledge him,
and he will make straight your paths. (Proverbs 3:5-6, ESV)

So do not fear, for I am with you;
do not be dismayed, for I am your God.
I will strengthen you and help you;
I will uphold you with my righteous right hand. (Isaiah 41:10, NIV)

Praise be to the God and Father of our Lord Jesus Christ, the Father of compassion and the God of all comfort, who comforts us in all our troubles, so that we can comfort those in any trouble with the comfort we ourselves receive from God. (2 Corinthians 1:3-4, NIV)

Cast all your anxiety on him because he cares for you.

Be alert and of sober mind. Your enemy the devil prowls around like a roaring lion looking for someone to devour. Resist him, standing firm in the faith, because you know that the family of believers throughout the world is undergoing the same kind of sufferings.

And the God of all grace, who called you to his eternal glory in Christ, after you have suffered a little while, will himself restore you and make you strong, firm and steadfast. (1 Peter 5:7-10, NIV)

Prayer

Lord Jesus Christ, it would have been enough if you had just brought us together, but you have gotten us through many challenges and blessed us in many ways. We thank you for your constant providence. We wait with expectant hope for you to make your presence known to us in strong and unmistakable ways as we face our present difficulties.

Comfort us, Lord. Console us. Help us stand strong together through it all and to remember to take care of each other even when we're stressed and scared. Above all, help us respond to this challenge in a way that gives you glory and lets the world see you at work in our lives. And ultimately lead us to the resurrection that comes after this cross. Amen.

CHAPTER NINE

Praying about Your Romantic Life and Intimacy

Let him kiss me with kisses of his mouth,
for your love is better than wine. . . .
Your name is a flowing perfume—
therefore young women love you.
Draw me after you! Let us run!
The king has brought me to his bed chambers.
Let us exult and rejoice in you;
let us celebrate your love: it is beyond wine!
Rightly do they love you! (Song of Songs 1:2-4)

Love between a husband and wife is meant to be free, total, faithful, and fruitful—reflecting the love that comes from God's own heart. No part of your relationship is untouched by God's grace. Too often we think of our bodies as base and of passion and sex as dirty, but Christians should not look upon these gifts from God the way the pagans do.

St. John Chrysostom, a Doctor of the Church, had some thought-provoking things to say regarding the awkwardness some Christians feel about integrating their sexuality with their faith:

Why are you blushing? Leave that to the heretics and pagans, with their impure and immodest customs. For this reason I want marriage to be thoroughly purified, to bring it back again to its proper nobility. You should not be ashamed of these things. If you are ashamed, then you condemn God who made marriage. So I shall tell you how marriage is a mystery of the Church!

As Greg discusses in his book *Holy Sex! A Catholic Guide to Toe-Curling, Mind-Blowing, Infallible Loving,* sacraments make the common holy. Simple water becomes the water that births new children of God. Common oil becomes the instrument that conveys our dignity in Christ. Simple bread and wine become Christ's Body and Blood. Each of these things is more shocking than the last.

For some people, the Church's understanding of marriage is equally shocking: after a man and woman promise themselves to one another in holy matrimony, they consummate that promise with their bodies. As the *Catechism* says, the bond of marriage "results from the free human act of the spouses and their consummation of the marriage" (1640).

In Christian marriage, sex is much more than recreation. It is a re-creation of the wedding vows by which sex is sanctified and empowered to become an efficacious sign—that is, an outward sign of a deeper reality and the cause of that deeper reality—that bears witness and simultaneously empowers the two to become one.

Through lovemaking, the married couple is granted certain blessings. First, as mentioned, the two literally become one. Second, they are given the power to co-create life with

God, not just through conception, but by joining each other in the commitment to form and raise their children together. Finally, they are honored to be a physical sign of the passionate love God holds in his heart for each of us.

Although the average Christian is not used to thinking of sex in these terms, it is how the Church tells us we must think of it. Just as the "stuff" of baptism is water and the "stuff" of the Eucharist is bread and wine, the "stuff" of marriage is the very body of the man and the very body of the woman and the physical love they share.

Christianity is an incarnational faith that demands an embodied response. This is one of the reasons behind the monastic tradition of celibacy. Historically, men and women who were serious about living their Christian faith sought to give their whole selves to Christ—soul, mind, *and body*. Celibate monks and religious don't renounce their sexuality; they give it to God so that God may sanctify it and allow them to be spiritually generative, with their lives dedicated to prospering the unity of the Church and fostering new life in the Church.

But, as St. John Paul the Great's writings teach us, God wants an embodied response, not only from monks and nuns, but from everyone. The more Christian couples dedicate their physical love to Christ and seek to live in accordance with the teachings of the Church regarding sexual practices, the more they embrace the "universal call to holiness" and access the grace that allows them to become saints.

Seen in this light, how could a couple choose *not* to pray about their romantic and sexual relationship? Clearly, there is more going on in the bedroom than meets the eye. How could we expect to create this kind of love on our own power, using only the knowledge the world can give us through Hollywood and the Internet? We can't.

Making marital sexuality sacred and prayerful does not make it boring, stodgy, puritanical, timid, or tentative. It does exactly the opposite. Read the Song of Songs, which various Church fathers and saints have said mirrors God's love for us. The Song of Songs is an epic poem of two lovers who are driven to such distraction that no danger or social convention, such as the inadvisability of a woman going out alone at night to seek her lover, could stand in its way. The passion between the two lovers is so all-consuming that it would be scandalous if it was not ordained by God.

Daughters of Jerusalem, I charge you—
if you find my beloved,
what will you tell him?
Tell him I am faint with love. (5:8, NIV)

Let us go early to the vineyards
to see if the vines have budded,
if their blossoms have opened
and if the pomegranates are in bloom—
there I will give you my love. (7:12, NIV)

How handsome you are, my beloved!
Oh, how charming!
And our bed is verdant! (1:16, NIV)

Your mouth [is] like the best wine.

May the wine go straight to my beloved,
flowing gently over lips and teeth! (7:9, NIV)

His mouth is sweetness itself;
he is altogether lovely.
This is my beloved. (5:16, NIV)

Your lips drop sweetness as the honeycomb, my bride;
milk and honey are under your tongue. (4:11, NIV)

I have taken off my robe—
must I put it on again? (5:3, NIV)

My beloved is to me a sachet of myrrh
resting between my breasts. (1:13, NIV)

My beloved has gone down to his garden,
to the beds of spices
to browse in the gardens
and to gather lilies. (6:2, NIV)

Blow on my garden,
that its fragrance may spread everywhere.
Let my beloved come into his garden
and taste its choice fruits. (4:16, NIV)

My lover put his hand in through the opening:
  my innermost being trembled because of him.
I rose to open for my lover,
  my hands dripping myrrh:
My fingers, flowing myrrh
  upon the handles of the lock. (5:4-5)

Open to me, . . .
  my dove, my perfect one!
For my head is wet with dew. (5:2)

God desires that you and your spouse experience this kind of passion because, wonderful though it might be in earthly terms, it is merely a drop in the well of passionate love God holds in his heart for you. God's love is not in the least bit sexual, of course, but it is unquestionably *nuptial*. Scripture makes it clear: as the bridegroom desires to be completely one with his bride, God desires to be completely and totally united with us.

Greg's book *Holy Sex!* goes into more detail about how you can live the fullness of this love on a practical level. For now it is enough to look at how you might begin to consecrate your romantic love to Christ and allow God's grace into your love life, not to extinguish the fires of your passion for one another but to pour new, godly fuel on the fire.

As we have said repeatedly throughout this book, there are many ways to pray. What is important is that you pray from the heart. In whatever manner works best for you, bring this part of your relationship to the Lord.

Reflection Questions

- Does it seem odd, offensive, upsetting, or off-putting to think that God wants you to pray about your romantic and sexual life? If so, what do you think you have to gain by working through this resistance?
- How might bringing your romantic and sexual relationship to God in prayer challenge the way you think about sex and romance?
- Do you think it would make a difference in your romantic love if you allowed grace to play a larger role? Why or why not?

Daily Prayer for Romantic Life

It is not unusual for spouses to feel a little disconnected from one another throughout the day. Between work, children, and our million and one responsibilities, it can be hard to keep the fires of romance burning brightly. In addition to reflecting on the Song of Songs, as well as on Scripture passages about God's love for us, consider offering up a little prayer asking God if you could borrow a little of his passionate love. Ask him to help you remember that before you were hard-charging go-getters in the workplace, and before you were supermom and superdad, you were lovers.

Lord, in spite of all the busyness of this day, set my heart on fire with your passion for my spouse, and give us the energy we need to act on that passion. Let us continue to be the joyful gifts to each other that you have always intended us to be.

You can use this prayer, or something like it, anytime throughout the day but especially when you are feeling a little disconnected, lonely, or burned out. Reach out to the passion in God's heart, and then do something, even something small, to reach out to your spouse. Just as God multiplied the five loaves and two fish, he can multiply the meager scraps of passion you have left after a long day of work and kids.

Reflection Questions

- How might remembering to pray about your romantic life once or twice throughout your day shift your focus toward your spouse?
- If you were to pray about your romantic life, what graces do you think God might give you, enabling you to do things differently in your marriage?

Take God on a Date

Couples rarely get the opportunity to go on dates at the rate everyone says they should. For most couples, it isn't practical or even possible. And then there's reality: when you finally do get to go out, how often do you and your spouse end up frustrated because you talked mostly about the kids, had different expectations for the date, or fought the whole time—who knows why?

Sounds like a little grace might be in order, no? On those occasions when you do get to go out together, while you're still sitting in the driveway before leaving, give your date to God:

Lord, thank you for this time to be together, time to remember that we're friends and lovers in addition to parents and partners. Help us to have an enjoyable time reconnecting with each other and to be patient and gentle with each other as we move out of mommy and daddy mode and rediscover the love and passion we have underneath it all.

We give you the most intimate parts of our relationship all over again and ask you to help us use this time well, so that our love for each other may glorify you and refresh our hearts. Amen.

Using this prayer, or something in your own words, helps you remember to lay the pressures of life aside, let God be in charge of your time together, and let him help you be who he needs you to be for each other.

The Lover's Prayer

Perhaps the most intimate way to give your romantic love to God is to develop what we like to call a "lover's prayer."

Don't worry; we aren't suggesting that you kneel on oppo-
site sides of the bed and pray a Rosary before lovemaking.
But there is nothing wrong—and a lot right—with asking
God to help you experience the passion spoken of in the
Song of Songs. A passion rooted in truly loving each other.
A passion that doesn't use or take advantage of each other.
That passion that Pope Benedict XVI wrote will "rise 'in
ecstasy' towards the Divine."[13]

A lover's prayer could be prayer on your own or together
each day, as a way of remembering that you are called to be
signs of God's passion to one another. It can also be prayed,
alone or together, before being intimate, as a way of asking
God to make your love purer and more passionate.

Praying through Frustration

Sometimes, even when couples love each other very much
and desire each other even more, things just don't work
out. You're too sick or exhausted. A child knocks on the
door right when you think the coast is clear. Or you need
to take several days off from making love because you are
using Natural Family Planning and are trying to avoid a
pregnancy.

These things always seem to happen at the worst possible times, when you feel that you need each other the
most. These times are hard to deal with under the best of
circumstances. It's easy to give in to pouting, sniping, or
passive-aggressive little digs, pushing each other even further away and making it harder to get back in sync.

The world believes that there is no value in suffering. But Christians, who are called to relieve suffering in whatever moral ways we can, also recognize that when there is no getting around suffering, God is still present. He will help us learn something about ourselves and others through the pain.

It's important to remember this when dealing with the sexual frustration couples not uncommonly feel in marriage, for whatever the reasons. In those times, try praying together instead of turning on each other or trying to white-knuckle your way through your frustration. Remember that your spouse will be healthy and rested again; you will reenter the infertile phase; you will resume relations.

Lord, we wish that we could be completely together today; it's hard to avoid becoming frustrated. We long for the comfort of each other's bodies, to feel safe, to feel loved, and to feel cherished. Even though we can't be sexually intimate today, help us be fully intimate with each other in every other way that is good, and right, and godly.

Help us resist the temptation to pout or withdraw or be irritable or use each other in any way. Let us instead put our whole selves into growing in the virtues that help us truly live for each other rather than for ourselves. Help us care for each other, love each other, cherish each other, and reassure each other of how truly important we are to each other. Even in our frustration, help us remember to look for ways to be your most precious gift to each other today and every day.

Will this prayer (or a similar prayer of your own design) take away all the frustration you feel at not being able to be together on a given day? Of course not. But it certainly will help. It reorients the struggle. It reminds you that rather than one of you being the supplicant and the other the gatekeeper, you are in this struggle together. And it helps you connect with the grace to see what blessings and growth God may wish to bring about in you through this time of sexual separation rather than in spite of it.

When You Aren't "Feeling It"

Sometimes the problem isn't sexual frustration but rather the loss of desire. Greg deals with the psychological and relational dimensions of this problem in *Holy Sex!* This issue can provoke spiritual challenges that are rooted in guilt, anger, self-hatred, discomfort with one's body, past trauma, or simply garden-variety exhaustion or temporary illness.

Even these times can help you draw closer to God and to each other. Here is an example of one way you might pray through these feelings, draw closer to your spouse in spite of these feelings, and when necessary, find the courage to seek help in order to overcome more serious challenges to your intimate life.

Lord, I know that you have given me to my spouse to be a physical sign of your passionate love, but right now I'm having a hard time living up to that. Help me resist the temptation to beat up on myself, to feel broken or insufficient, or to lash out in anger when my spouse desires me. Instead help me be as generous as I can be in loving my spouse in all the ways that are possible and appropriate, even while I set whatever limits I must to protect my health and well-being.

Ultimately though, renew my desire. Restore my energy. Help me overcome any emotional, physical, or relational obstacles that stop me from being the gift you mean for me to be. Heal me; if necessary, give me the courage to seek help to facilitate that healing. Give me the health, the rest, and the mindset that will allow me to love my spouse fully and without reservation.

Again, while this prayer will not necessarily bring about a spontaneous healing of everything that is negatively impacting your romantic relationship, it recasts the struggle, recognizing both your right to attend to your own well-being and your commitment to love each other freely, totally, faithfully, and fruitfully.

Reflection Questions

- How might praying specifically about the challenges of your sexual relationship change the way you and your spouse view this part of your marriage?
- If you were to open your frustrations and challenges to God in prayer, how might it change the way you and your mate relate to each other?

Infertility and Miscarriage

Primary or secondary infertility affects about 10 percent of all married couples and is a particularly painful experience. Miscarriage, too, though medically common, can be personally devastating. We have experienced both of these challenges in our relationship, so we know the struggles they can entail emotionally, spiritually, and relationally.

With infertility as with miscarriage, husbands and wives may find themselves dealing with their grief in very different ways, which can make it hard for them to feel as if they are in it together. This is why, for instance, couples who have experienced infertility or miscarriage have a 20 percent greater risk of separation and divorce than do other couples. And with miscarriage, about 15 percent of couples (both men and women) experience serious emotional turmoil that can involve depression, anxiety, and phobias about sex related to the fear of losing another pregnancy.

Infertility and miscarriage are obviously very real struggles that call for serious attention and an extra measure of grace. But having struggled with these issues in our own marriage, we have come to discover God's presence in the midst of the pain. Through God's mercy and our persistent commitment to praying together, we ultimately drew closer to one another through the pain. Many of the suggestions we have already made in the chapters on discernment and praying through hardships are applicable here, but we wanted to make a special mention of these issues because of the unique challenges they can present to a couple's romantic and sexual relationship.

We strongly recommend that couples struggling with infertility seek the anointing of the sick. Contrary to persistent popular opinion, this is not a sacrament reserved for the terminally ill. It is a sacrament of healing, intended to communicate God's grace to those who are suffering from physical or emotional illness. It offers a powerful way for couples to connect with the healing grace of Christ.

Further, the Elizabeth Ministry (ElizabethMinistry.com) offers wonderfully faithful and effective resources and support to couples and individuals struggling with infertility, miscarriage, stillbirth, and a host of related issues. Their work can be a great blessing to couples as they connect with the spiritual support of others who are facing similar challenges.

Beyond this, we hope the following prayers might inspire you to find your own way of praying through these challenges:

Prayer during Infertility

Lord, our hearts ache for a child. We feel so alone, so frustrated, so angry, disappointed, and confused. Help us. Despite our pain, help us find ways to reach out to each other, to love each other, to support each other, and to comfort each other through this awful time.

Help us grow closer as we struggle together to find your will, grace, and meaning through this trial. Be present to us, Lord. Console us. Help us respond to this pain in a way that glorifies you and leads us to the answers we seek. Jesus, we trust in you. Amen.

Prayer in Miscarriage

Lord, we are devastated. Words can't begin to express our grief, our pain, our anger, and our anguish. Please, God, "out of the depths [we] call to you" (Psalm 130:1). Hear us. Help us. Give us the grace we need to be truly present and loving to each other through our grief and despite our pain. Help us draw closer to you even though we are hurting and feel abandoned by you. Help us feel your presence and hold on to your love in the midst of this devastation.

Give us the consolation we are seeking. Help us find our way to the resurrection that comes after this cross. Jesus, we place our trust in you.

May these prayers inspire you to find your own words and your own ways to cling to God and each other through these trials. Know that you are close to our hearts and in our prayers as well.

Conclusion

There is no part of your life that God wants to leave untouched by his grace, including the most intimate core of your marriage. Do not be ashamed of the body God gave you and the ways he has created you to love one another through your body. As St. John Chrysostom said:

> *And how become they one flesh? As if you should take the purest part of gold, and mingle it with the other gold; so in truth here also the woman as it were receiving the richest part fused by pleasure, nourishes it and cherishes it, and throughout contributing her own share, restores it back to the man.*

Let God be the Lord of the love you share. And may every expression of your love for one another fill your hearts with God's own passion, allowing you to "rise in ecstasy toward the Divine" (*Deus Caritas Est, 5*).

Listen to His Word

Alone or with your spouse, ask God to let his word in Scripture speak to you throughout the day. Post the following verses in various prominent places, so you can find strength and consolation in God's word when you need it most.

Let your fountain be blessed and have joy of the wife of your youth,
your lovely hind, your graceful doe.
Of whose love you will ever have your fill,
and by her ardor always be intoxicated. (Proverbs 5:18-19)

The husband should give to his wife her conjugal rights, and likewise the wife to her husband. For the wife does not rule over her own body, but the husband does; likewise the husband does not rule over his own body, but the wife does. Do not refuse one another except perhaps by agreement for a season, that you may devote yourselves to prayer; but then come together again. (1 Corinthians 7:3-5, RSVCE)

The LORD God said: It is not good for the man to be alone. I will make a helper suited to him. (Genesis 2:18)

The man said:
"This one, at last, is bone of my bones
and flesh of my flesh;
This one shall be called 'woman.'" (Genesis 2:23)

The man and his wife were both naked, yet they felt no shame. (Genesis 2:25)

Let marriage be held in honor among all, and let the marriage bed be undefiled. (Hebrews 13:4, RSVCE)

Prayer

Lord Jesus Christ, you have given us to each other as husband and wife, so that we can become one in you and through our love for one another. We give our bodies to you. We consecrate our love and passion for each other to you. We ask you to use our bodies as they were created to be used: to love each other, to work for each other's good, to build each other up, to encourage each other to share in the free, total, faithful, and fruitful love that flows from your own heart, that we might "rise in ecstasy towards the Divine" through your grace and mercy.

We thank you for the joy, pleasure, and comfort we find in each other's arms, and we ask that you would help us be a sign of your passionate love for us, that we might glorify you even in the most intimate part of our life together. We pray this in the name of Jesus Christ our Lord. Amen.

CHAPTER TEN

The Power of a Prayerful Couple

"I have the power to lay down my life, and I have the power to take it up again. No one takes it away from me; but I lay it down of my own accord, that I may take it up again" (Jn 10.18.17). They disturbed him, but he lay down to sleep.

In this respect Adam was a type of Christ. God sent a deep sleep upon Adam, in order to fashion a wife for him from his side. Was God unable to make a wife for the first man by taking her from his side while he was awake? . . . Because in Christ's case, a bride was made for him as he slept on the cross, and made from his side. With a lance his side was struck as he hung there, and out flowed the sacraments of the Church.

—St. Augustine, Enarrationes in Psalmos, 56[14]

Marriage is more than a source of earthly comfort. It is more than an accessory to be acquired and then laid aside. It is more than something created for the present moment. Christian marriage is your ministry, both to one another and to the world at large. It is the path of your sanctification. It is itself a prayer. It is one of the most beautiful ways God will use your lives to give the world a tangible witness to the love that everyone longs for but few dare to believe is real in this age. If you will let him, if you give every part of your relationship to him—the good, the bad, the joyful and sorrowful, the celebrations and the struggles—he will use it all to help you fulfill the destiny for which you were created: total, joyful, and eternal union with him.

If you get nothing else from this book, we hope you take away two things. First, we hope that you see that there is more to marriage than meets the eye. Let the world think of marriage as a convenience, a nice thing to have, or an aggravation or hindrance. You know better. Marriage is a blessing and an opportunity for spiritual growth, a life-changing experience, a community-building enterprise, a grace-filled ministry, and a powerful sign of God's love in the world.

A marriage that is little more than a guaranteed date for bowling night may not deserve much time, attention, or energy, but the marriage we've described in these pages certainly does. Value your marriage. Treasure it. Give it the time, energy, and importance it deserves, so that it can be the transformative, spiritual enterprise—the sacrament—God means for it to be.

Second, we hope you understand that God is interested in every part of your marriage. Every single moment of your marriage is worth praying about, either with your spouse or on your own—not simply so that you can beg God for help or thank him for blessings, but so that you can hear him speaking to you. We hope we have helped open your eyes to the spiritual power churning just beneath the surface of even the most mundane moments of your everyday lives. Those moments are packed with spiritual power, teeming with grace.

When your spouse asks you to do that somewhat-out-of-character thing—go fishing with him, for example, or go with her when she volunteers at the homeless shelter—you need to hear the voice of God, saying, "This is how I want you to grow." When your spouse asks you for help with the dishes, or the kids, or a work problem, or an emotional struggle, God is saying, "Will you help me?" When you argue, God is saying, "I've heard what you both want, but would you like to hear what my plan is for both of you?"

There is real power in being a prayerful spouse and more in being a prayerful couple. It is the power to know that it's OK that you don't know how to love each other the way you need to—at least not yet. It is the power to know that when you're unsure what love requires of you next, you can go to God and ask him and trust that he will lead you, step-by-step, so that you get where you need to go.

It is the power to know that you are loved beyond measure and that you don't have to "settle" in your marriage. For even if your marriage is a struggle, God can help you and your spouse become a witness to the world of all he can do when two broken people turn to him and say, "Teach us."

It is the power to take your joys, frustrations, celebrations, struggles, and every great and small moment shared between you and your spouse and dedicate them to a higher purpose—that of winning the crown of eternal life and becoming the saints you were meant to be.

Heaven doesn't start at some point in the distant future. It starts now. And you can see glimpses of it in the love shared between you and your spouse. Just as bread and wine don't look like much on their own but, when consecrated, become the food of the angels; just as water is water until it is consecrated to God and becomes the spring of eternal life—just so, your marriage might not seem like much in the eyes of the world, but in the eyes of God, you are a sign to the world of his love.

You don't have to be perfect. In fact, it's better that you're not. As St. Paul says, "I will all the more gladly boast of my weaknesses, that the power of Christ may rest upon me" (2 Corinthians 12:9, RSVCE). The only thing it takes is a heart that is willing to pray for and (ideally) with your spouse. A heart that turns to God every day and says,

Give me the courage to share your passion, your desire, and your longing for my spouse. Give me the commitment to be more vulnerable, more honest, more faithful, more intimate, more joyful. Help me work harder for my spouse's good, even when that asks more from me than I'd prefer to give. Help me say and do the hard things my spouse needs me to say and do, so that I can be more faithful to you and call my spouse on to deeper faithfulness to you.

Take our marriage, whatever it is today, and make it what you want it to be for tomorrow and every day, until we meet you face-to-face at the eternal wedding feast.

An Invitation from the Authors

We hope that this book has helped affirm you in the ways you are already reaching out to God in your marriage and helped you discover a few new ways you can bring God more into your everyday life and love.

Through the Pastoral Solutions Institute (www.Catholic-Counselors.com, 740-266-6461), we offer ongoing support to help you achieve the goals outlined in this book—from telephone-based spiritual direction and pastoral counseling; to hundreds of free self-help videos; to More2Life, our daily call-in radio program; to our free weekly e-letter; to hundreds of other books, articles, quizzes, and resources that can give you the tools you need to celebrate the life God wants to give you.

If we can be of any further support to you and your spouse, we hope you will call on us and our associates. You are part of the body of Christ, so you don't ever have to struggle alone. Let us be your Simon of Cyrene, to lighten your burden and help you experience God's grace through the trial and the cross, to the resurrection that surely comes.

May the grace and peace of Jesus Christ be with you and with all those you love.

Dr. Greg and Lisa Popcak

Endnotes

1. Pope Benedict XVI, Deus Caritas Est, Encyclical Letter on Christian Love, 5, Vatican.va

2. Pope Francis, Address to the Course on the Marriage Process, February 25, 2017, Vatican.va.

3. St. John Vianney, Catechetical Instructions: Sermons, as quoted in Robert Atwell, Celebrating the Saints: Daily Spiritual Readings to Accompany the Calendars of the Church of England, the Church of Ireland, the Scottish Episcopal Church, and the Church in Wales (London: Canterbury, 2017), 292.

4. Pope John Paul II, General Audience, November 7, 1979, Vatican.va.

5. Pope Benedict XVI, "Prayer Opens the Way to the Mystery of God's Plan," General Audience, June 20, 2012, http://www.catholicculture.org/culture/library/view.cfm?id=9999.

6. Lewis Block Jerrold, Sheldon Harnick, "To Life" (Warner/Chappell Music) from the movie Fiddler on the Roof.

7. St. Augustine paraphrase, from Sermon on 1 John 4:4-12.

8. See Vatican II, Gaudium et Spes, Pastoral Constitution on the Church in the Modern World, 24.

9. You can learn more at www.CatholicCounselors.com

10. U.S. Catholic Bishops, Catholic Household Blessings and Prayers: A Companion to the Catechism of the Catholic Church (New York: Image, 2012), 48.

11. Eli Finkel, The All-or-Nothing Marriage: How the Best Marriages Work (New York: Penguin, 2017), 190.

12. St. Thomas Aquinas, Summa Theologiae, I, question 1, article 8, reply to objection 2.

13. Pope Benedict XVI, Deus Caritas Est, Encyclical Letter on Christian Love, 5, Vatican.va.

14. St. Augustine, "Exposition of Psalm 56," in Expositions of the Psalms, trans. Maria Boulding, OS.B., ed. John E. Rotelle, O.S.A. (New York: New City, 2001), vol. 17, 111-112.